OFFICIAL FORTNITE
HOW TO DRAW 2

L B

CONTENTS

DRAWING FIGURES

Drawing human figures can be a tricky skill to master. To create the cool Outfits in this book, you'll need to draw a character to wear them! Let's take a look at how to start drawing human bodies.

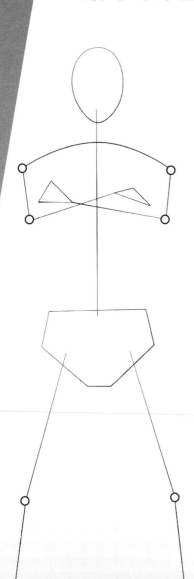

FRAME

Don't dive straight into the details. Always begin with a simple stick figure. A strong framework at this stage will help you capture your character's pose. Joint alignment rarely changes on the body, so lightly marking the placement of each joint with a small circle at this early stage will help to keep your entire figure in proportion.

Human figures are usually eight "heads" tall. It can help to carefully sketch a series of evenly spaced horizontal lines across the page to keep your figure's proportions correct.

TOP ART TIP!

Use a light hand when sketching so your guidelines are easy to erase.

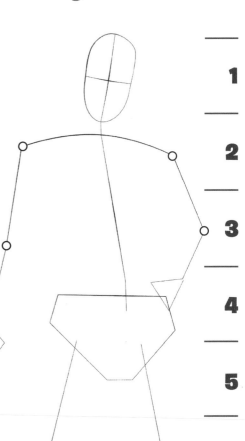

1
2
3
4
5
6
7
8

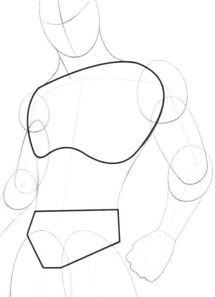

TOP ART TIP!

Start with the head if you're struggling. Sketching the body's shape will become second nature in no time!

OUTLINE

With your figure in place, begin building form around your framework. The human body can be broken down into a series of basic shapes. Ovals and cylinders form most parts of the body.

When outlining the torso, it can help to separate the rib cage, stomach, and pelvis into individual shapes rather than one solid outline. While the shape of the ribs and pelvis will rarely change, the stomach will vary depending on the character's body type.

TOP ART TIP!

Practice sketching lots of stick figures in different poses to get comfortable with the structure of the body.

FACES

Placing facial features can be difficult. Sketch in construction lines to help you: a horizontal line for the eyes and a vertical line for symmetry. Take care to ensure your character's features line up properly.

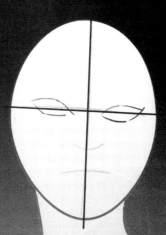

Start with the eyes. They create a lot of expression, so experiment with shape and size until you have the right fit for your character. For human figures, there is usually one eye's distance between the eyes.

REMEMBER!

These are all guidelines. The step-by-step illustrations in this book are there to help you, but don't be afraid to go rogue and have fun drawing your character!

PERSPECTIVE

Drawing an object straight on doesn't always make for a very interesting illustration. People and objects can look different depending on the angle we view them from. Height, distance, and pose can all impact perspective. A good understanding of this technique will give your drawings depth and help to create a 3-D appearance. Here are a few tips to get you started.

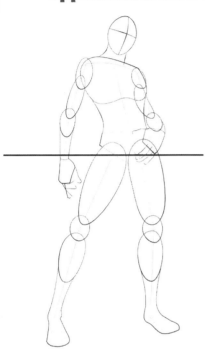

THE HORIZON LINE

Perspective is generally built around the horizon line. This is simply the viewer's eye level, where your own eye is drawn to when looking at an image. The placement of this line can draw attention to a particular area of your drawing.

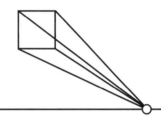

One-point perspective is a simple way to prevent your drawing from looking flat. On a blank piece of paper, try sketching a horizon line. Draw a dot in the middle of the line. This is your vanishing point. Draw a square above the line, then connect each corner to the vanishing point. The shape appears to get smaller as it nears the horizon line. This is perspective.

FORESHORTENING

Foreshortening creates the illusion of 3-D space in a 2-D drawing. For example, different poses can distort a character's body and make limbs look longer or shorter than if we were looking at the figure head-on. Your sketch may seem a little crooked to begin with, but using correctly marked joints as a guide will ensure your character's dynamic pose looks proportional when firming up your outline.

TOP ART TIP!

Begin by determining your horizon line. This will help you visualize which body parts will appear larger/closer, and which will seem smaller/farther away.

Take care when foreshortening. A limb farther away from our line of sight might appear shorter but the width doesn't change. Watch out for overly skinny arms to compensate for the short length.

Overlapping can create a foreshortened drawing. When sketching your character's outline, draw each shape in full, even if it will be covered later by clothing or another body part. This will help you to keep your proportions correct and create a more realistic perspective.

TOP ART TIP!

Always begin by determining your drawing's vanishing point. Building around this point will help to create perspective and keep everything in proportion.

SHADING

Cast shadows are a great way to create the illusion of depth. Gradating value adds shape to your object or character, giving it a strong 3-D look. Carefully consider how shadows form around the shape of your drawing.

LIGHT SOURCE

Identifying your light source is the first key step to impactful shading as it dictates where highlights should be used and where shadows should fall.

HOW TO DRAW:
BLACK SHIELD

TOP ART TIP!
If you're struggling to get the shield's proportions right, try sketching a kite shape then rounding the lines to create the curved edges.

1 Begin drawing Black Knight's Legendary Back Bling by lightly sketching a shield shape.

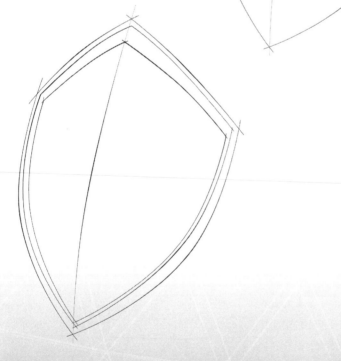

2 Draw two smaller shield shapes within your initial outline. The top and bottom points of each shape should line up with the central guideline.

3 Lightly sketch the outline of the shield's reinforcements at the Back Bling's base and outer edges.

4 In the center of your shield, lightly sketch the outline of the fire-breathing dragon. The main body of the dragon follows the shape of the number 5 with the flat top acting as the creature's lower jaw.

5 Once you're happy with your dragon's outline, firmly pencil in the overall shape with thick blacks. Use rough lines to create dents in the metal.

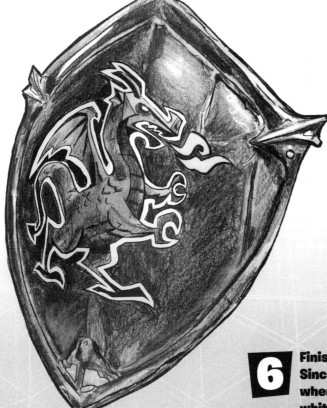

TOP ART TIP!

Don't be afraid of using really dark values. A full range of tones will make your drawing pop!

6 Finish by adding lots of value to Black Shield. Since the Back Bling is dark, use heavy lines when shading, leaving a few bright spots of white to create dynamic highlights.

HOW TO DRAW:
BRITE BAG

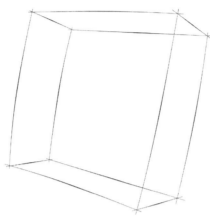

1

Pack a smile into this awesome Back Bling! Start with a light sketch of a large cube.

2

Begin defining Brite Bag's shape, curving the edges. Since the Back Bling is made of flexible material, your lines don't need to be too neat or straight.

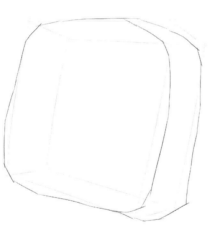

4

Add the zipper on Brite Bag's side. Use long straight lines to draw the rabbit's face on the zipper. Add fluff around its cheeks with short V-shaped lines.

3

Carefully sketch the handles and fabric strap. Use thin rectangles and consider how the material will fall.

5 Begin adding depth to the front of the Back Bling by layering squares within your outline. Keep the corners soft and curved.

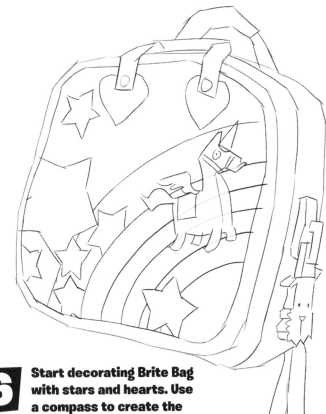

6 Start decorating Brite Bag with stars and hearts. Use a compass to create the rainbow's semicircular arches and sketch the unicorn's outline.

7 Firm up your pencilwork and erase any rough lines. Add a hexagonal pattern to the fabric strip and lightly outline the zipper's teeth. Apply heavy shading to the darkest areas of Brite Bag.

8 Continue adding value to your drawing. Blend your lines to create a smooth transition between shaded areas, sweeping a blending stick along the strokes. Brushes or tissue can be used, too.

11

HOW TO DRAW:
DEEP FRIED

1

Begin drawing this tasty Back Bling by sketching a wide cuboid.

TOP ART TIP!

Don't rush through the sketching stage. Starting with a strong outline will make it easier when you begin adding detail.

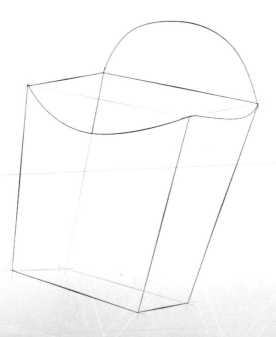

2 Using your initial guidelines, sketch a semicircle at the top of the Back Bling. Lightly curve the the front and right side of the carton.

3 The carton's outline doesn't need to be too neat. Use short, rough lines to give it a crumpled appearance. Add a rough circle in the center of the Back Bling.

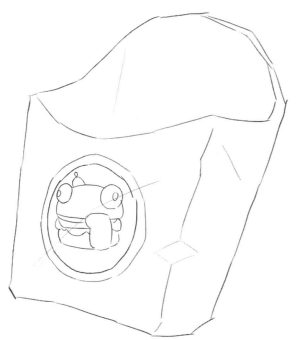

4 Sketch Beef Boss's logo in the center of the circle. The face can be broken down into a series of circles, semicircles, and ovals.

5 Fill the carton with fries. Draw a random series of long, thin cuboids at varied lengths and angles to make the Back Bling seem stuffed full!

TOP ART TIP!

Though the logo is small, detail goes a long way. Clearly define the different parts of the burger with thick lines. Draw rough circles on top of the bun and darkly shade the pupils.

6 Mark light dents on the carton before adding value to your perfectly greasy Back Bling. Use flat grays for the carton. Vary the shading on each of the fries, adding spots of highlights.

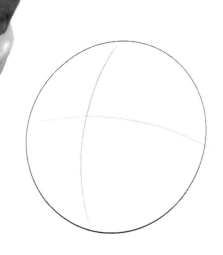

HOW TO DRAW:
HATCHLING

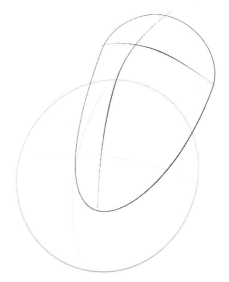

1 To create this baby bag, use a compass to lightly draw a wide circle. Add curved horizontal and vertical central guidelines.

2 Layer a wide oval shape on top of your initial circle. This will become the triceratop's face.

3 Erase any part of the oval shape which overlaps with Hatchling's lower half. Draw a large circle around the Back Bling's face and two smaller ovals to mark the position of its paws.

4 Lightly sketch Hatchling's defining features. Use cone shapes to outline the horns and claws. Add an eye and a thin smile, and mark the bony neck frill's sections with short, curved lines.

5 Use your guidelines to start defining the Back Bling's overall shape. Draw small diamonds, squares, and pentagons to add detail to the base of the eggshell.

6 Use thick black lines to firmly mark Hatchling's outline and erase any remaining guidelines. Use light lines to mark the spots on the dinosaur's skin.

TOP ART TIP!

Use the side of a mid-weight pencil tip when shading Hatchling's body, varying pressure to create a mottled texture.

7 Before roaring into action, add a light touch of value to your Back Bling. Draw attention to Hatchling's horns and claws with dense blacks.

HOW TO DRAW:
POOL PARTY

1

Loosely sketch a long oval to start drawing this magically floaty Back Bling.

2
Outline the long neck and facial shape by penciling in a tall, thin cuboid and a trapezoid along the upper half of the neck.

3
Add Pool Party's unicorn horn, long mane, and curved tail. Lightly sketch the Back Bling's eye and handle placement.

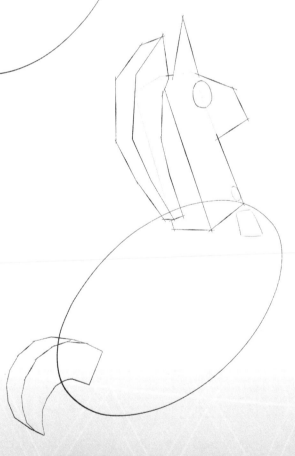

4 Begin defining the Back Bling's features, adding an ear, pupil, and the lower jaw. Perspective will make the muzzle appear short. Sketch a small oval in the center of the floaty's body and add two small oval legs. Erase any remaining guidelines.

TOP ART TIP!
Avoid using rigid, straight lines to give the Back Bling a fully inflated look.

5 Add definition to Pool Party by lightly penciling in lines around its circular body, as well as on its horn, tail, and mane.

TOP ART TIP!
Shade with neat, even strokes to make blending easier. Overlapping the lines will prevent any visible gaps.

6 Firmly outline your drawing. Finish by adding value to the Back Bling. Start with a layer of gray and gradually layer shadows on top. Use an eraser to create white highlights on the inflatable material.

17

HOW TO DRAW:
RAPTOR SATCHEL

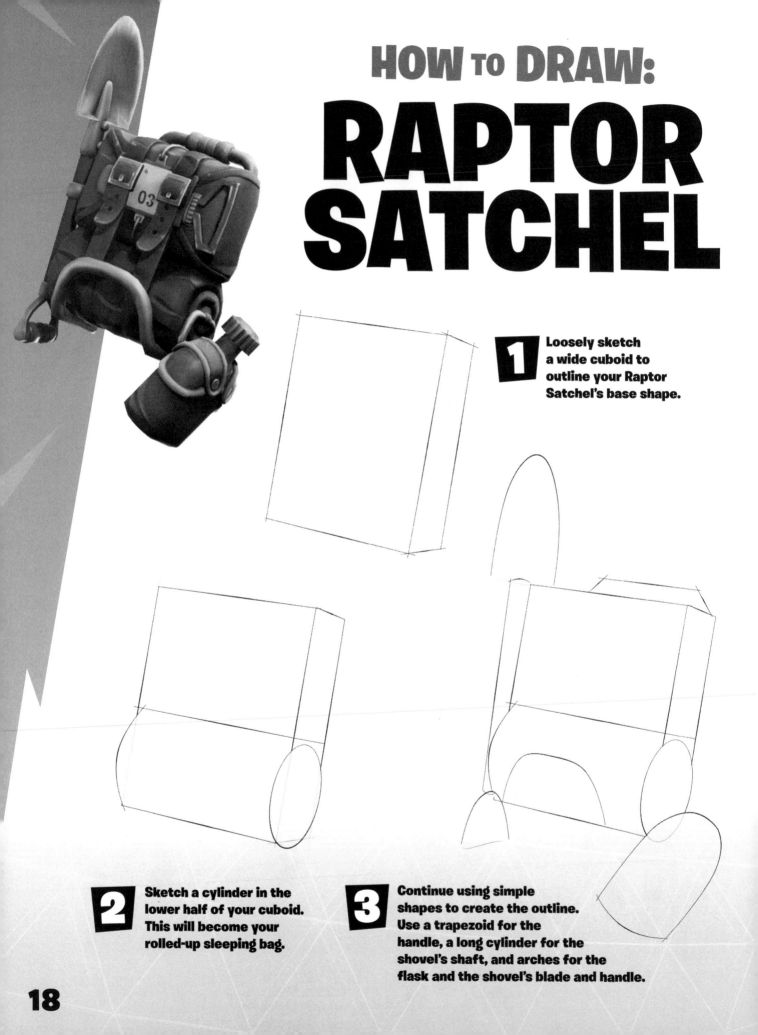

1 Loosely sketch a wide cuboid to outline your Raptor Satchel's base shape.

2 Sketch a cylinder in the lower half of your cuboid. This will become your rolled-up sleeping bag.

3 Continue using simple shapes to create the outline. Use a trapezoid for the handle, a long cylinder for the shovel's shaft, and arches for the flask and the shovel's blade and handle.

4 Start adding definition to the Back Bling. Add straps to the backpack and a cap on the flask. Pencil in the shovel's sockets and the blade's step.

5 Begin firming up your drawing's outline and add finer details, including buckles. Add folds and rolls in the Back Bling's fabric.

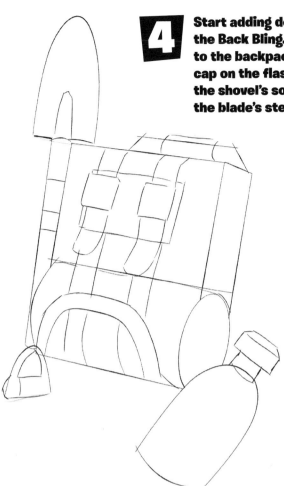

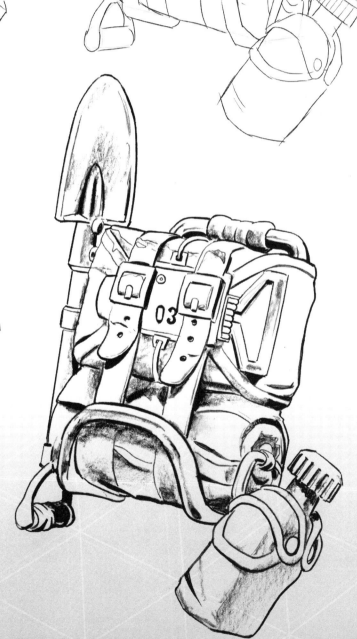

TOP ART TIP!

Use your shading to help define shape. Varying the direction of your shading can help to add to your drawing's perspective and create depth.

6 Add the number 03 in thin lettering. Finish by adding a light touch of value to your standard issue Back Bling. Carefully consider how you use your pencil strokes to reflect the Raptor Satchel's different materials.

HOW TO DRAW:
BONESY

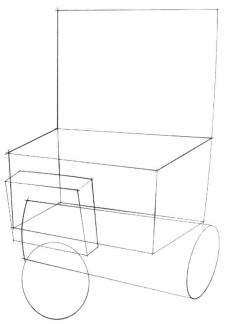

1

Start with a light sketch of the Back Bling's outline. Bonesy's carrier can be broken down into simple rectangles, circles, and cylinders.

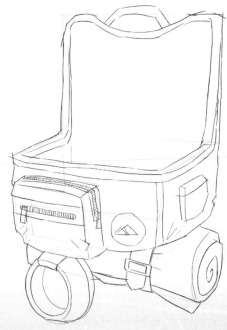

2 Begin defining the Back Bling's shape, softening the edges of the carrier. Add curves to the sleeping bag. Sketch placement for the round badge and square side pocket.

3 Build upon your guidelines to add detail to the carrier. Lightly sketch a handle and add rolls to your sleeping bag. Use short, rough lines to create a zipper effect along the front pocket. Use a series of circles to add depth to the dog bowl.

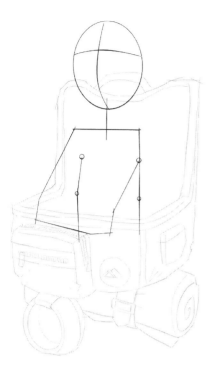

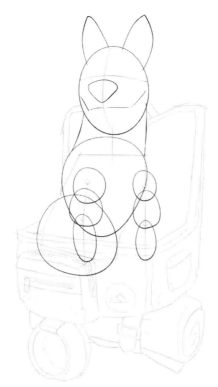

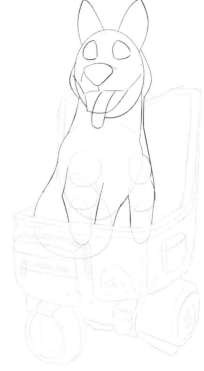

4 It's time to start sketching your loyal companion. Begin with a light framework of Bonesy's upper body.

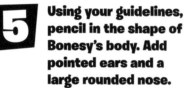

5 Using your guidelines, pencil in the shape of Bonesy's body. Add pointed ears and a large rounded nose.

6 Sketch Bonesy's outline. Since his fur isn't too fluffy, some muscle definition will be visible. Pencil in the facial features.

7 Firm up Bonesy's outline and add defining features. Use his eyes and eyebrows to create a bright, smiley expression. Don't forget his bandana!

8 Finish your good boy Back Bling by adding dark value to key areas of your drawing. Use subtle strokes when outlining Bonesy's body. This will create a furry appearance without having to shade all of Bonesy.

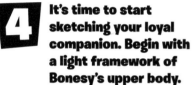

21

HOW TO DRAW: STARCREST SHIFT

1 Use simple lines to sketch the rough base shape of this elegantly engineered Back Bling.

2 Lightly pencil in a cube in the center of your sketch's upper crossline.

3 Build simple shapes around your cube to create the main body of your Back Bling. Sketch a trapezoid at the top and a curved cuboid at the bottom, sitting on top of an H shape.

4 Begin defining the shape of Starcrest Shift's curved wings. Add an arch in the center of the H shape. Soften the edges of your Back Bling's main body.

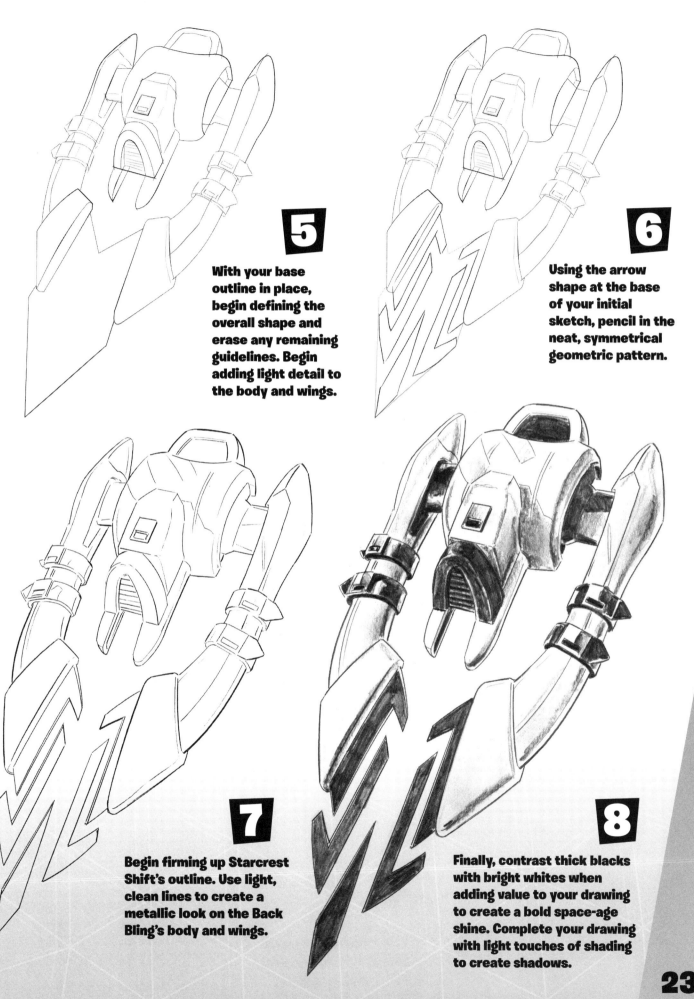

5

With your base outline in place, begin defining the overall shape and erase any remaining guidelines. Begin adding light detail to the body and wings.

6

Using the arrow shape at the base of your initial sketch, pencil in the neat, symmetrical geometric pattern.

7

Begin firming up Starcrest Shift's outline. Use light, clean lines to create a metallic look on the Back Bling's body and wings.

8

Finally, contrast thick blacks with bright whites when adding value to your drawing to create a bold space-age shine. Complete your drawing with light touches of shading to create shadows.

HOW TO DRAW: DUAL PISTOLS

1

Start by lightly sketching the outline of one pistol, using rough cuboid shapes. Leave a gap in your outermost lines to mark positioning for your second pistol.

2

Add a second outline in front of your initial sketch, filling in the gap from step 1. Once again use cuboids for the outline.

3

Erase any unnecessary guidelines and lightly mark the placement for each pistol's muzzle and sight, and the ejection port on the fully visible weapon.

4

With the base frame of your weapons established, begin to define the shape of your pistols. Curve the grip's outline and sketch the shape of the trigger and barrel.

5 Continue adding definition to your drawing, including diagonal markings on the barrel's side and small ridges underneath. Lightly pencil in finger grips on each handle.

6 Once you're happy with the shape of your pistols, firmly pencil in the outline and details. Erase any rough linework.

TOP ART TIP!
Soft graphite pencils are best for shading. They can easily blend to create smooth surfaces.

7 Add value to your drawing using low-contrast shading for a metallic shine. As light is hitting the front pistol, it casts a shadow onto the second gun. So use heavier values when shading the partially covered pistol to create a 3-D look.

25

HOW TO DRAW: SEMI-AUTO SNIPER RIFLE

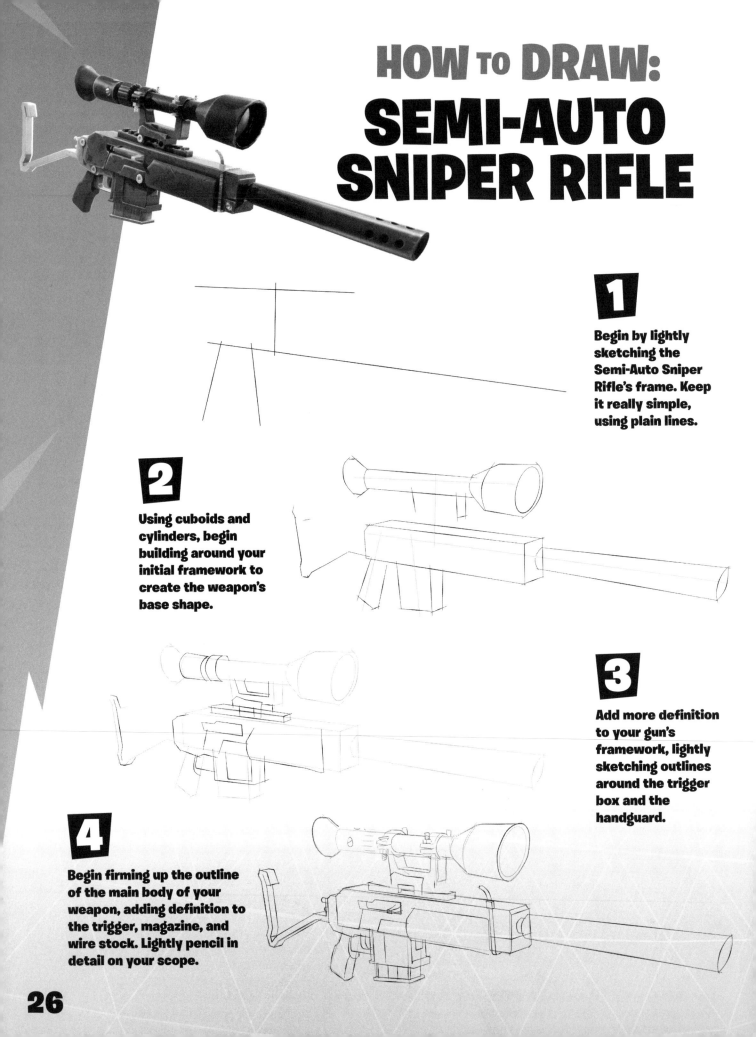

1

Begin by lightly sketching the Semi-Auto Sniper Rifle's frame. Keep it really simple, using plain lines.

2

Using cuboids and cylinders, begin building around your initial framework to create the weapon's base shape.

3

Add more definition to your gun's framework, lightly sketching outlines around the trigger box and the handguard.

4

Begin firming up the outline of the main body of your weapon, adding definition to the trigger, magazine, and wire stock. Lightly pencil in detail on your scope.

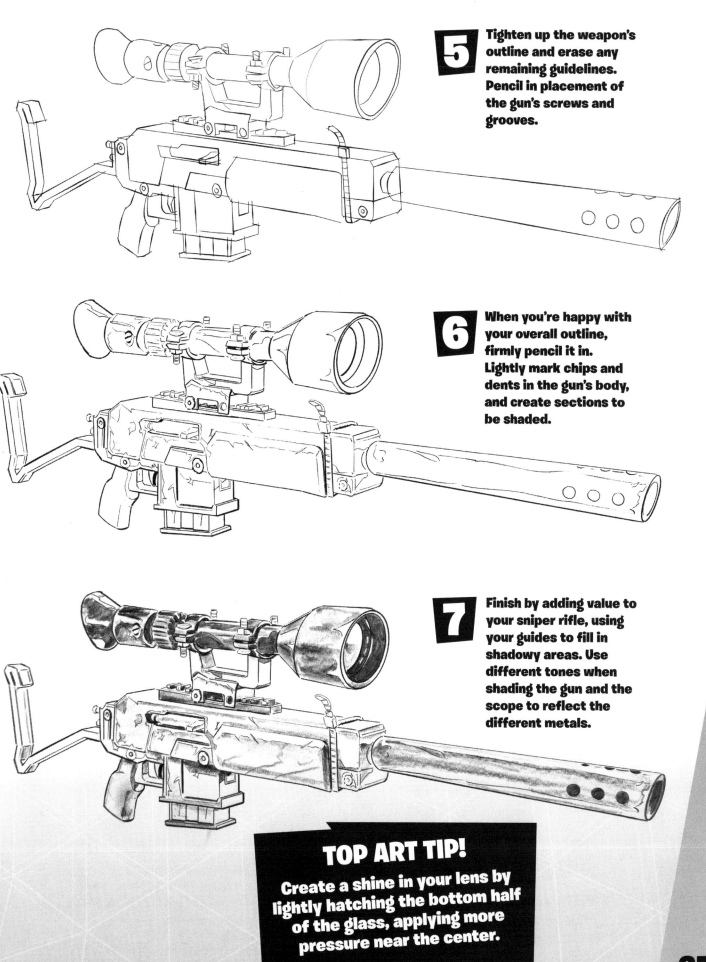

5 Tighten up the weapon's outline and erase any remaining guidelines. Pencil in placement of the gun's screws and grooves.

6 When you're happy with your overall outline, firmly pencil it in. Lightly mark chips and dents in the gun's body, and create sections to be shaded.

7 Finish by adding value to your sniper rifle, using your guides to fill in shadowy areas. Use different tones when shading the gun and the scope to reflect the different metals.

TOP ART TIP!
Create a shine in your lens by lightly hatching the bottom half of the glass, applying more pressure near the center.

HOW TO DRAW:
SUPPRESSED PISTOL

1 Make a simple start to the Suppressed Pistol by drawing a large L shape. The top line should be almost three times the length of the handle line.

2 Using simple lines, lightly sketch the weapon's framework. Use your ruler to help mark placements for the various sections. Combined, the hammer, muzzle, and suppressor should be the same length as the gun's main body.

3 Loosely add shape to your weapon, creating a curved underside, adding a front sight, and making the suppressor more rounded at each end.

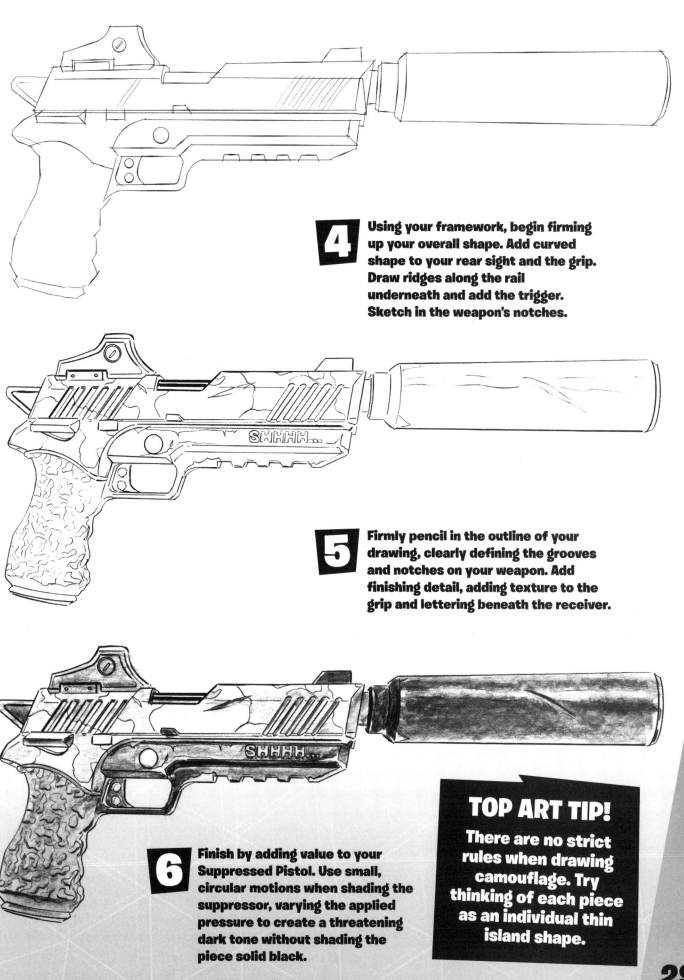

4 Using your framework, begin firming up your overall shape. Add curved shape to your rear sight and the grip. Draw ridges along the rail underneath and add the trigger. Sketch in the weapon's notches.

5 Firmly pencil in the outline of your drawing, clearly defining the grooves and notches on your weapon. Add finishing detail, adding texture to the grip and lettering beneath the receiver.

6 Finish by adding value to your Suppressed Pistol. Use small, circular motions when shading the suppressor, varying the applied pressure to create a threatening dark tone without shading the piece solid black.

SHHHH...

TOP ART TIP!

There are no strict rules when drawing camouflage. Try thinking of each piece as an individual thin island shape.

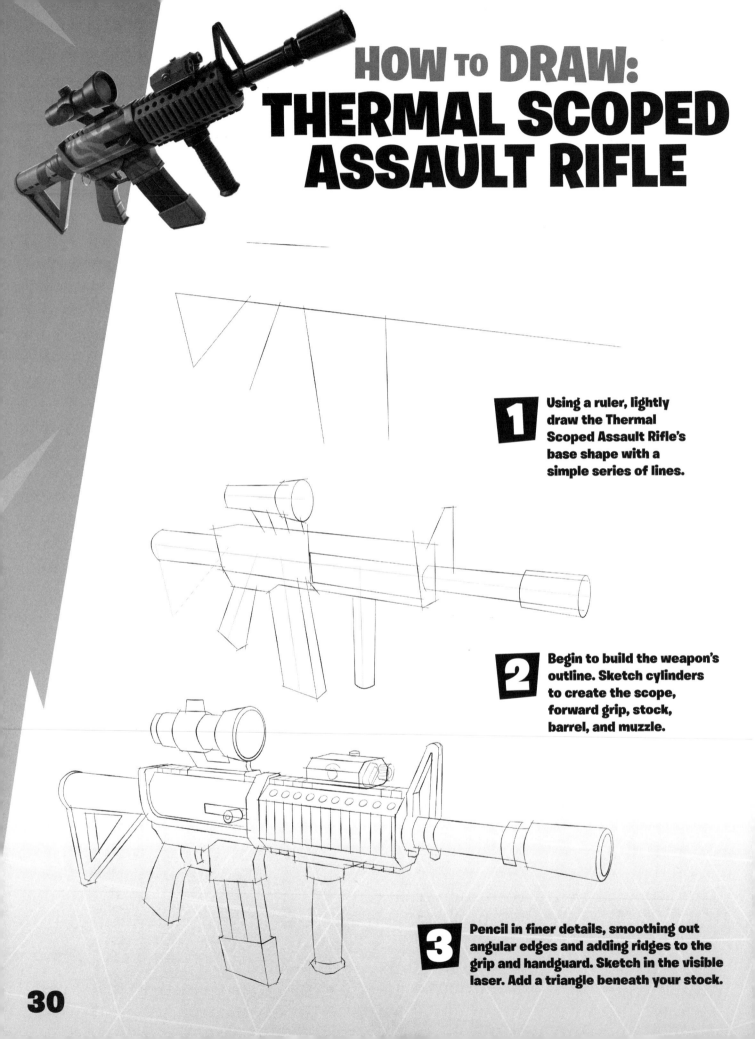

HOW to DRAW:
THERMAL SCOPED ASSAULT RIFLE

1 Using a ruler, lightly draw the Thermal Scoped Assault Rifle's base shape with a simple series of lines.

2 Begin to build the weapon's outline. Sketch cylinders to create the scope, forward grip, stock, barrel, and muzzle.

3 Pencil in finer details, smoothing out angular edges and adding ridges to the grip and handguard. Sketch in the visible laser. Add a triangle beneath your stock.

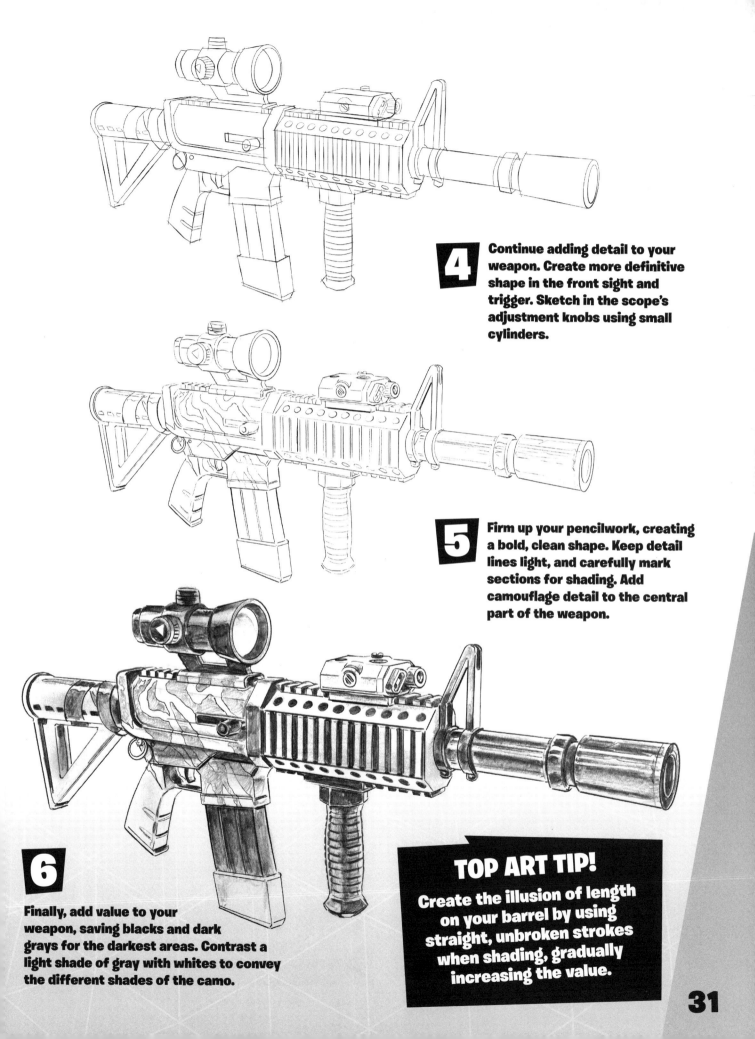

4 Continue adding detail to your weapon. Create more definitive shape in the front sight and trigger. Sketch in the scope's adjustment knobs using small cylinders.

5 Firm up your pencilwork, creating a bold, clean shape. Keep detail lines light, and carefully mark sections for shading. Add camouflage detail to the central part of the weapon.

6 Finally, add value to your weapon, saving blacks and dark grays for the darkest areas. Contrast a light shade of gray with whites to convey the different shades of the camo.

TOP ART TIP!
Create the illusion of length on your barrel by using straight, unbroken strokes when shading, gradually increasing the value.

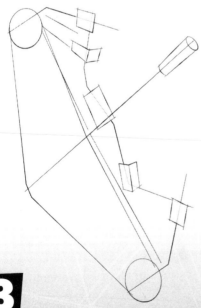

HOW TO DRAW:
BOOM BOW

1

Begin by lightly sketching simple straight lines to create your weapon's base shape.

2

Draw a circle at each end of the weapon, marking the position of the pulleys. Lightly sketch the Boom Bow's handle placement.

3

Add shape to the handle by sketching a series of small rectangles to outline the hinges. Add a cylinder at the tip of the arrow.

4

Continue to define the handle's shape. While it looks complex, the overall outline can be broken down into a series of cuboids and wedges.

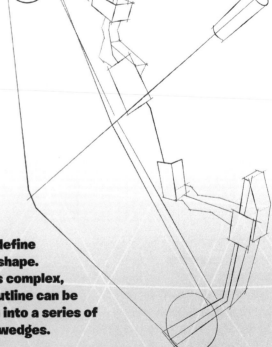

Using your guidelines, firmly pencil in Boom Bow's outline and begin to add finer detail to the handle, arrow, and pulley system.

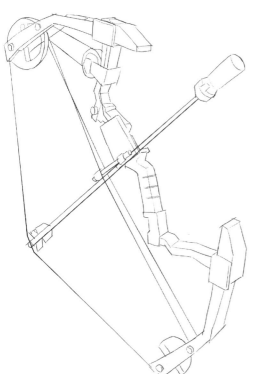

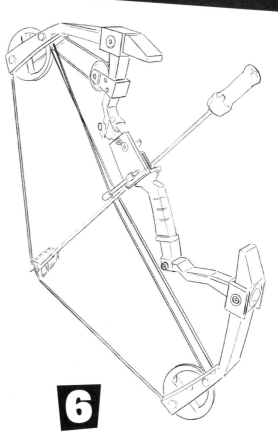

6

Thicken up the bow's strings, adding a second parallel line to each string. Draw the weapon's screws and bolts on the handle and pulley. Add definition to the tip of the arrow and a feathered texture to the fletching.

7

Before exploding into action with your Boom Bow, add light value to your drawing. Although the weapon is dark when in full color, save thick blacks for the bowstrings and arrow's shaft.

HOW TO DRAW: FALCON

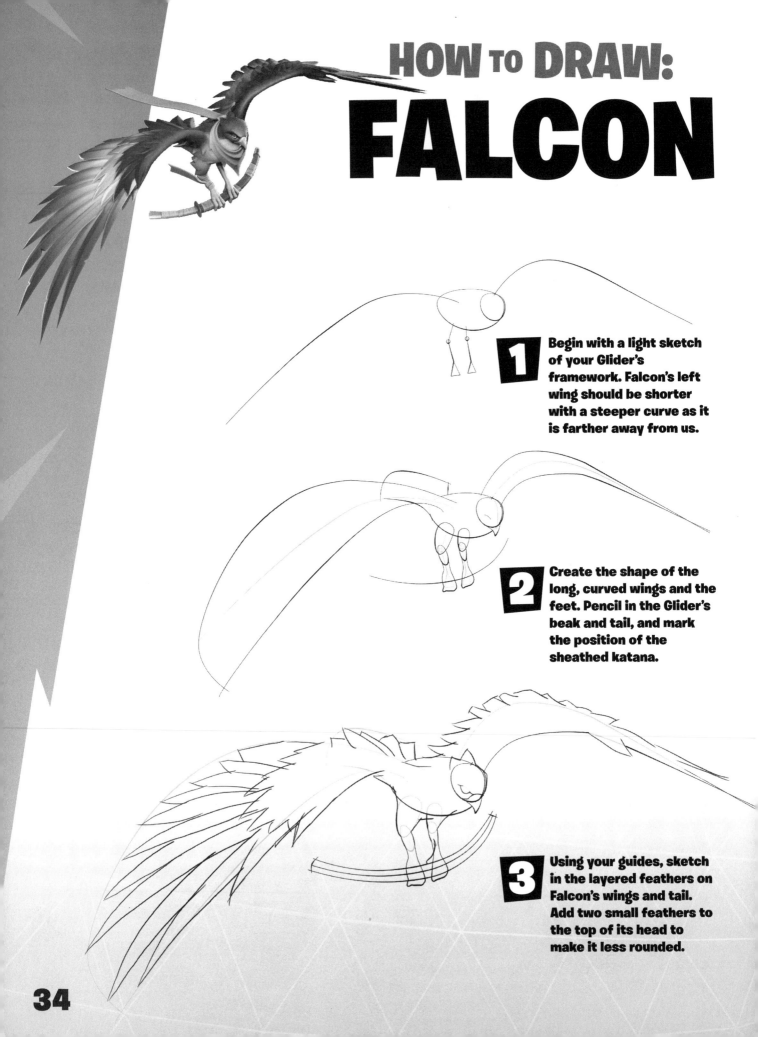

1 Begin with a light sketch of your Glider's framework. Falcon's left wing should be shorter with a steeper curve as it is farther away from us.

2 Create the shape of the long, curved wings and the feet. Pencil in the Glider's beak and tail, and mark the position of the sheathed katana.

3 Using your guides, sketch in the layered feathers on Falcon's wings and tail. Add two small feathers to the top of its head to make it less rounded.

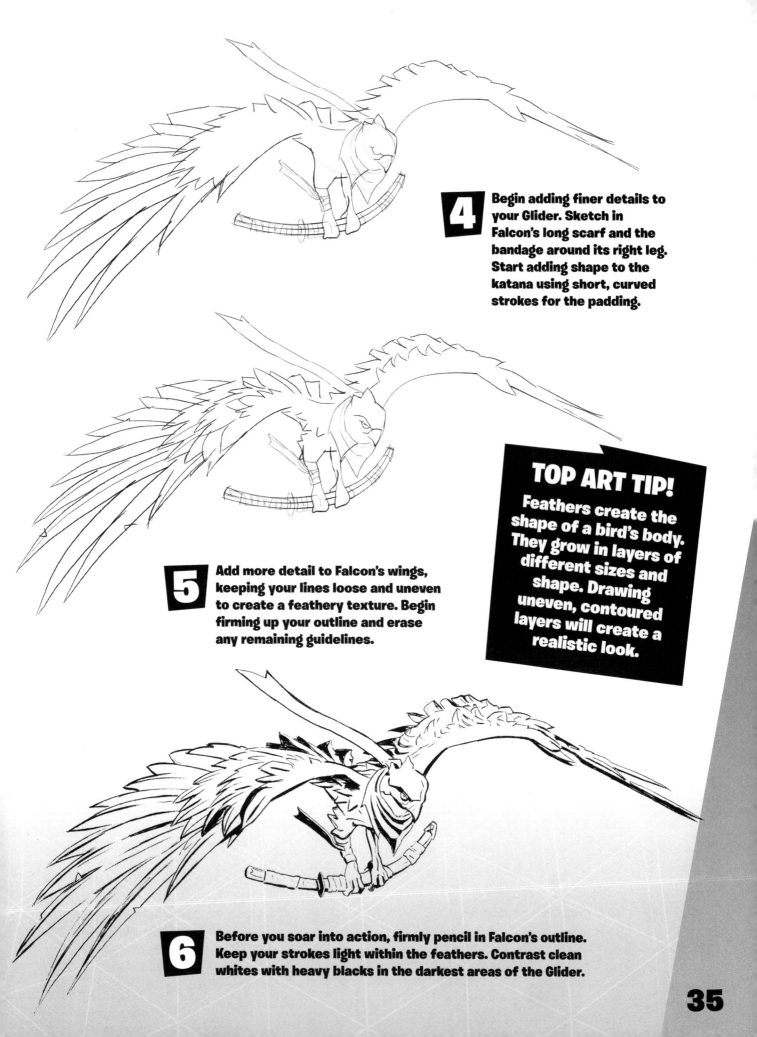

4 Begin adding finer details to your Glider. Sketch in Falcon's long scarf and the bandage around its right leg. Start adding shape to the katana using short, curved strokes for the padding.

5 Add more detail to Falcon's wings, keeping your lines loose and uneven to create a feathery texture. Begin firming up your outline and erase any remaining guidelines.

TOP ART TIP!
Feathers create the shape of a bird's body. They grow in layers of different sizes and shape. Drawing uneven, contoured layers will create a realistic look.

6 Before you soar into action, firmly pencil in Falcon's outline. Keep your strokes light within the feathers. Contrast clean whites with heavy blacks in the darkest areas of the Glider.

HOW TO DRAW: LASER CHOMP

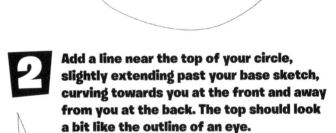

1 To draw this ferocious flying shark, start by sketching a large, uneven circle with a prominent peak on one side.

2 Add a line near the top of your circle, slightly extending past your base sketch, curving towards you at the front and away from you at the back. The top should look a bit like the outline of an eye.

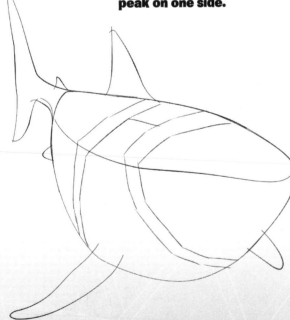

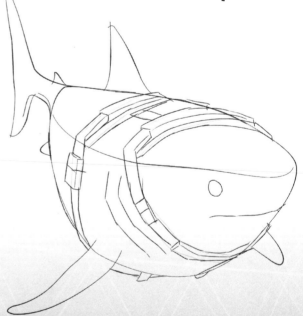

3 Building upon your base shape, sketch in your Glider's fins. Although Laser Chomp is a razor-sharp predator, you need to keep the angles of his fins soft. Mark the placement of his weapon's straps.

4 Begin adding detail to your shark. Pencil in a round eye and thin mouth. Use straight, angular lines for his gills. Add small, thin cuboids to the straps, creating buckles.

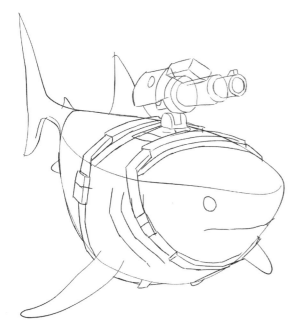

 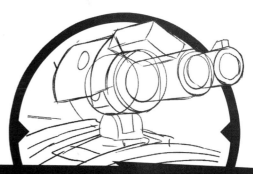

5

It's time to add the laser gun! Using your straps and dorsal fin as a guide, place the weapon's base in the center of the shark's back and draw the gun.

TOP ART TIP!

From the hinge upwards, the laser gun is made up of stacked cylinders.

TOP ART TIP!

Aside from a few light-gray shadows, leave the bottom of your shark white to accentuate the great white underbelly.

 6

With your weapon's shape in place, sketch in ridges around the barrel, with a long beam shooting out of the muzzle. Lightly mark the shark's underbelly with a rough line.

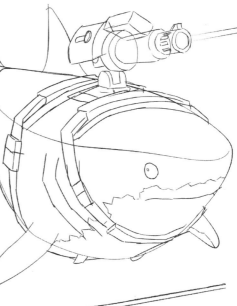

7

Add the Glider's handle and firmly outline your drawing with heavy lines. Shade your shark's body with different shades of light, flat grays, using thick blacks to accentuate his facial features.

HOW TO DRAW:
LAVAWING

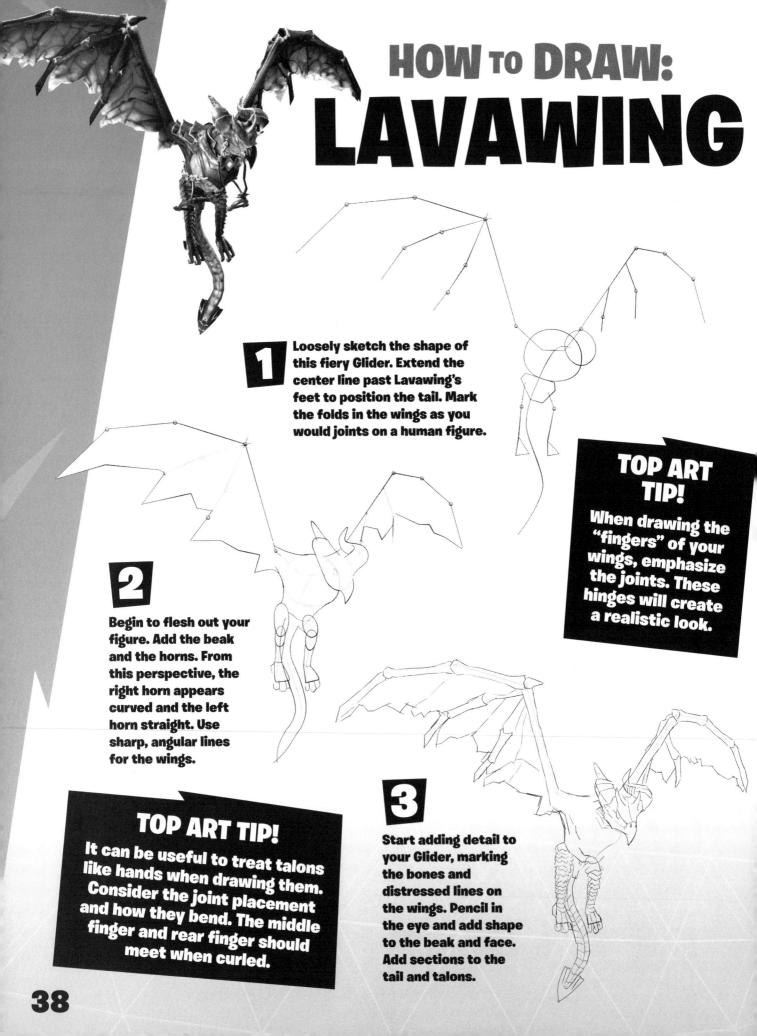

1 Loosely sketch the shape of this fiery Glider. Extend the center line past Lavawing's feet to position the tail. Mark the folds in the wings as you would joints on a human figure.

TOP ART TIP!

When drawing the "fingers" of your wings, emphasize the joints. These hinges will create a realistic look.

2 Begin to flesh out your figure. Add the beak and the horns. From this perspective, the right horn appears curved and the left horn straight. Use sharp, angular lines for the wings.

TOP ART TIP!
It can be useful to treat talons like hands when drawing them. Consider the joint placement and how they bend. The middle finger and rear finger should meet when curled.

3 Start adding detail to your Glider, marking the bones and distressed lines on the wings. Pencil in the eye and add shape to the beak and face. Add sections to the tail and talons.

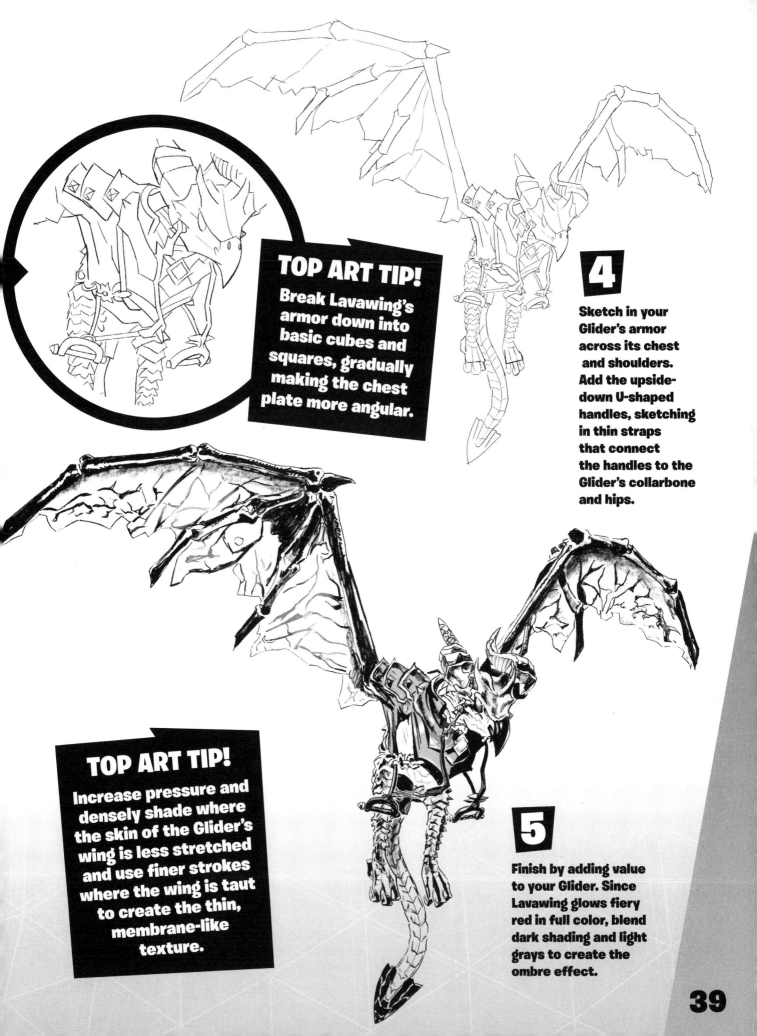

TOP ART TIP!

Break Lavawing's armor down into basic cubes and squares, gradually making the chest plate more angular.

4

Sketch in your Glider's armor across its chest and shoulders. Add the upside-down U-shaped handles, sketching in thin straps that connect the handles to the Glider's collarbone and hips.

TOP ART TIP!

Increase pressure and densely shade where the skin of the Glider's wing is less stretched and use finer strokes where the wing is taut to create the thin, membrane-like texture.

5

Finish by adding value to your Glider. Since Lavawing glows fiery red in full color, blend dark shading and light grays to create the ombre effect.

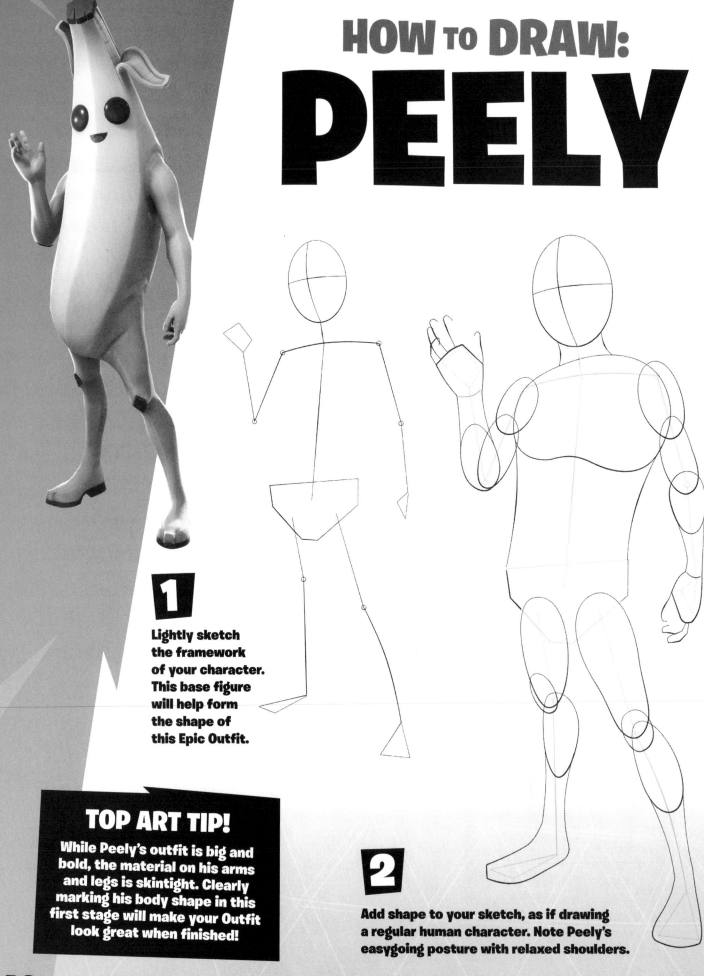

HOW TO DRAW:
PEELY

1

Lightly sketch the framework of your character. This base figure will help form the shape of this Epic Outfit.

TOP ART TIP!

While Peely's outfit is big and bold, the material on his arms and legs is skintight. Clearly marking his body shape in this first stage will make your Outfit look great when finished!

2

Add shape to your sketch, as if drawing a regular human character. Note Peely's easygoing posture with relaxed shoulders.

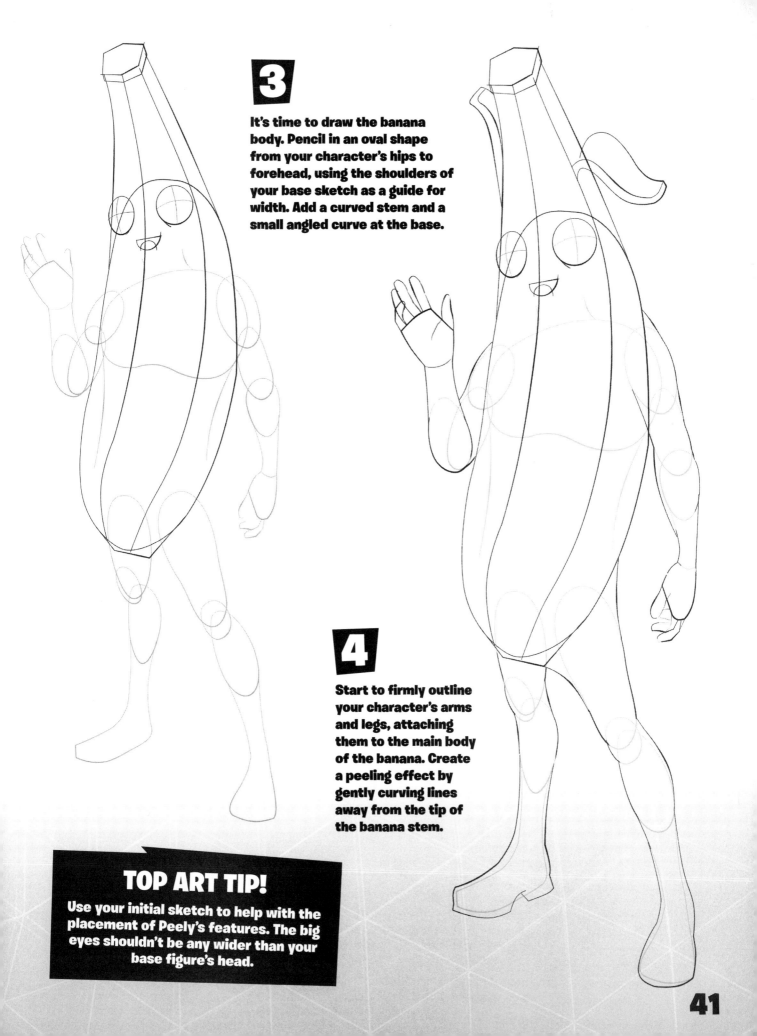

3

It's time to draw the banana body. Pencil in an oval shape from your character's hips to forehead, using the shoulders of your base sketch as a guide for width. Add a curved stem and a small angled curve at the base.

4

Start to firmly outline your character's arms and legs, attaching them to the main body of the banana. Create a peeling effect by gently curving lines away from the tip of the banana stem.

TOP ART TIP!

Use your initial sketch to help with the placement of Peely's features. The big eyes shouldn't be any wider than your base figure's head.

HOW TO DRAW: PEELY

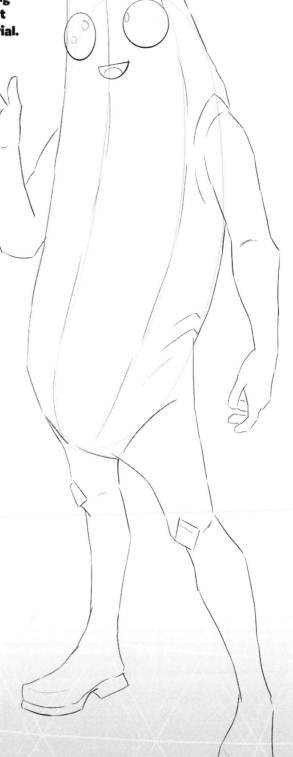

5

With the outline of your Outfit complete, firmly pencil in the overall shape of your character. Begin to add detail, including his kneepads and soft wrinkles in the material.

TOP ART TIP!

To capture bends in fingers, mark knuckle placement and work from there. Remember knuckles are not aligned in simple straight lines.

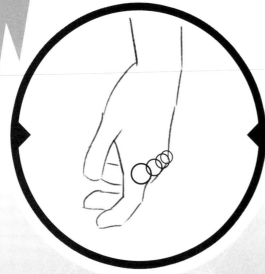

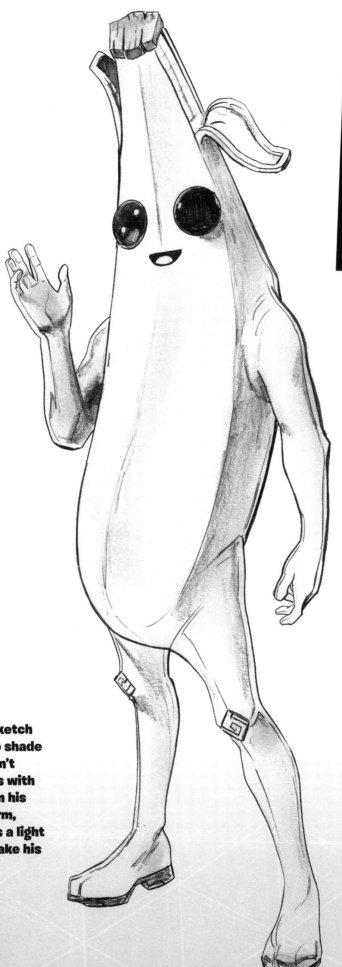

TOP ART TIP!

Emphasise Peely's friendly expression by using strong blacks for his eyes and mouth. Leave a couple of bright-white spots to create the glint in his eye.

6

Erase any visible sketch marks and begin to shade your Outfit. You don't need to go bananas with shading. Whether in his green or yellow form, Peely only requires a light touch of gray to make his curves stand out.

HOW TO DRAW:
BLACK KNIGHT

1 Begin drawing this Fort Knight by lightly sketching the character's base framework.

2 Start adding shape to Black Knight's body. His arms are crossed and his stance is wide as he stares directly at his target. His neck is quite thick, so carefully connect it to his broad shoulders.

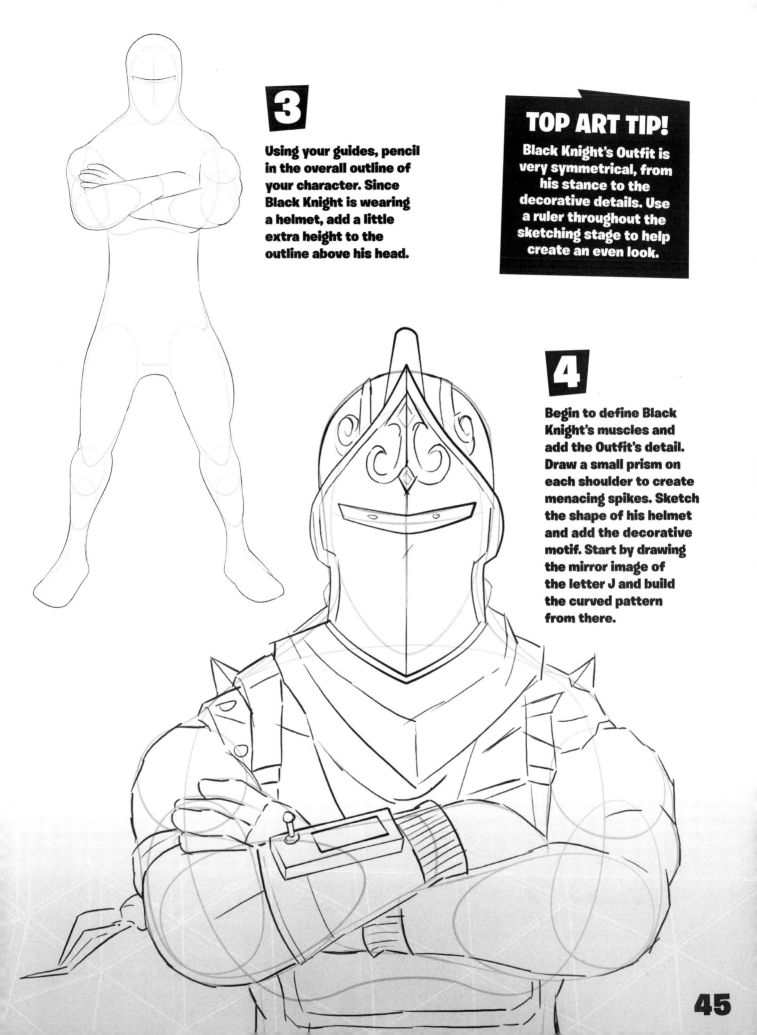

3

Using your guides, pencil in the overall outline of your character. Since Black Knight is wearing a helmet, add a little extra height to the outline above his head.

4

Begin to define Black Knight's muscles and add the Outfit's detail. Draw a small prism on each shoulder to create menacing spikes. Sketch the shape of his helmet and add the decorative motif. Start by drawing the mirror image of the letter J and build the curved pattern from there.

5

With Black Knight's upper body complete, firmly pencil in the detail for his lower body. The fabric of his pants doesn't fit tightly around his legs. Use angular strokes, particularly around his knees, to create defined shape.

TOP ART TIP!

Black Knight's belts sit just above his hips. Notice they gently curve upwards. Draw a long cuboid for his pouch, with the central line of your cuboid closely following the curve of your figure's torso guideline.

47

TOP ART TIP!

Add shading with intention. Plan where you will apply value and what strokes are best suited for the drawing. Try blocking in shadows first then define the highlighted areas.

6

Erase any remaining guidelines before shading your Outfit. Instead of using heavy blacks, contrast dark grays with bright whites to create a metallic shine on your helmet and shin pads. You're ready for battle!

HOW TO DRAW:
TRIPLE THREAT

1

Triple Threat is all about the fundamentals, so be sure to start with a sketch of her framework.

TOP ART TIP!

Although Triple Treat is pointing upwards, her finger isn't straight. Keep a light curve in her pointer finger and notice the downward slope of her folded knuckles.

2

Flesh out your initial figure, adding shape to her pose. Since she is standing at an angle, carefully consider how foreshortening will affect her left side.

3

Firmly pencil in the outline of your character's body, building upon your base sketch to shape her pointed finger and clenched fist. Lightly draw the outline of her eyes.

TOP ART TIP!

It can be tempting to draw wide-fitting shoes without guides. Sketching the shape of your character's foot will allow you to build your sneaker around it, keeping proportions correct.

4

Begin adding key details to her clothing, paying attention to the way her shirt falls loosely around her hips. Draw the main body of her hair, remembering to keep it in sections. Firmly pencil in the outline of her eyes.

HOW TO DRAW: TRIPLE THREAT

5 Start adding detail to Triple Threat's face and erase any visible guidelines. To draw her thick eyelashes, use one solid black line rather than drawing each lash individually.

TOP ART TIP!
Keep perspective in mind when adding the logo to Triple Threat's shirt. The letters will get smaller as they curve around her body.

TOP ART TIP!
When drawing a fist, it can be useful to start with the paddle shape of the palm and curl the fingers around it.

6 Move onto Triple Threat's clothing, adding the trim lines to her shorts and shirt. Light lines create texture on her socks. Add accessories and light lines to define her muscles.

7

Finally, add value to your drawing. The light source is angled above Triple Threat, creating shadows down the right side of her body. Take care to vary the pressure on your pencil to add dynamic highlights and dark shadows.

HOW TO DRAW:
DOGGO

1 Capture this good boy's pose by lightly sketching the body's framework. The head is rounder than an average human's and the eyeline should be placed in the upper third of the face.

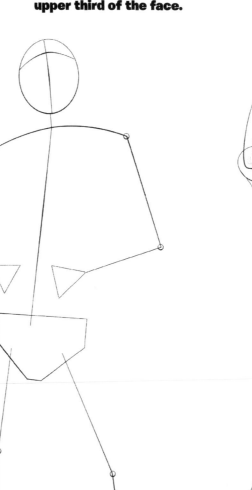

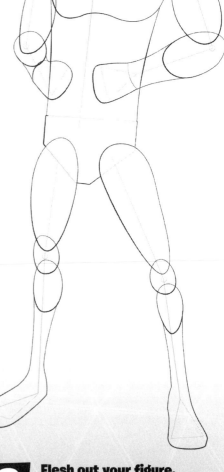

2 Flesh out your figure. Doggo is like a human with a pug's face, so drawing the shape of his body is just like drawing a male figure!

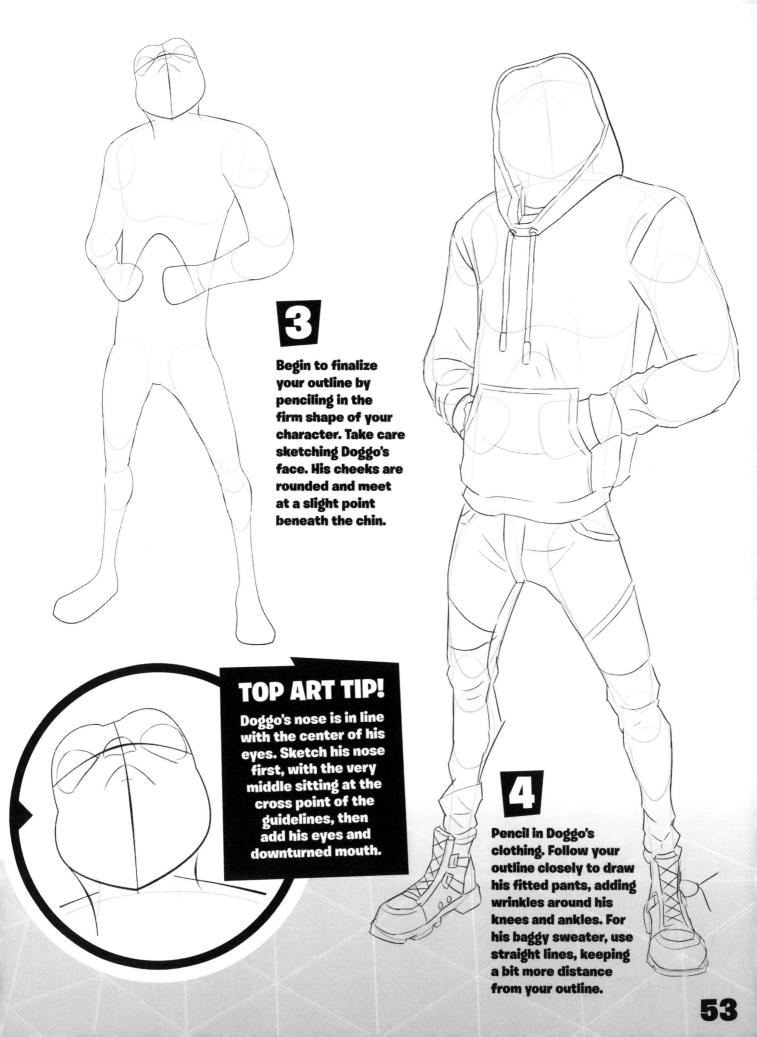

3

Begin to finalize your outline by penciling in the firm shape of your character. Take care sketching Doggo's face. His cheeks are rounded and meet at a slight point beneath the chin.

TOP ART TIP!

Doggo's nose is in line with the center of his eyes. Sketch his nose first, with the very middle sitting at the cross point of the guidelines, then add his eyes and downturned mouth.

4

Pencil in Doggo's clothing. Follow your outline closely to draw his fitted pants, adding wrinkles around his knees and ankles. For his baggy sweater, use straight lines, keeping a bit more distance from your outline.

HOW TO DRAW: DOGGO

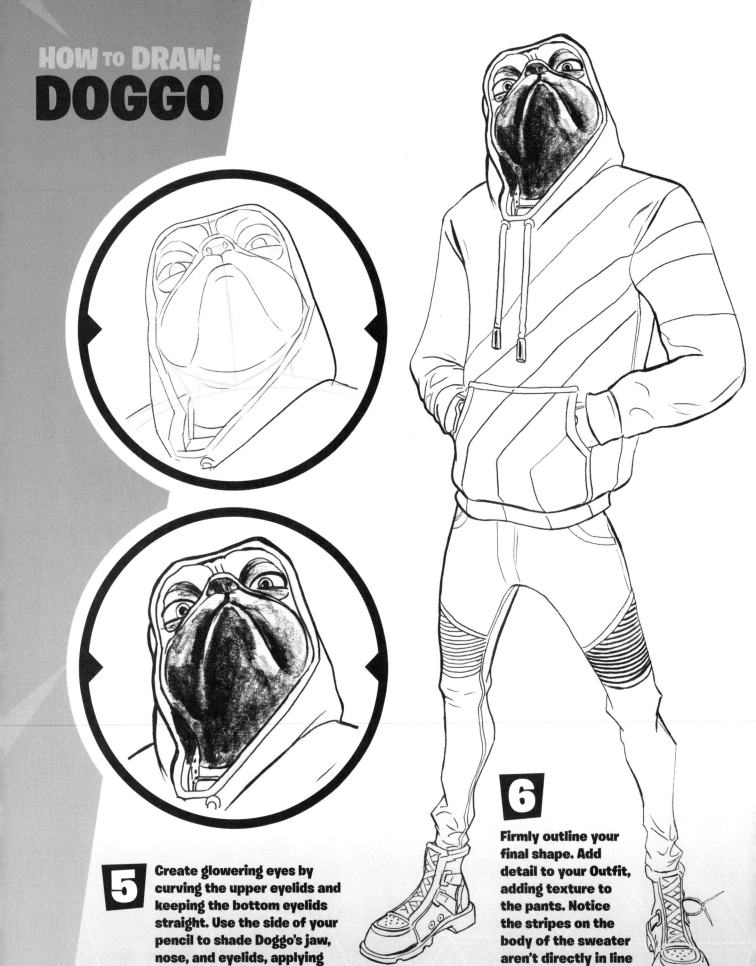

5 Create glowering eyes by curving the upper eyelids and keeping the bottom eyelids straight. Use the side of your pencil to shade Doggo's jaw, nose, and eyelids, applying more pressure where shadows fall.

6 Firmly outline your final shape. Add detail to your Outfit, adding texture to the pants. Notice the stripes on the body of the sweater aren't directly in line with the stripes on the arm.

TOP ART TIP!
Try to keep consistent pressure on your pencil while shading for a smooth, professional look.

7

Finish by adding value to your Outfit. Keep Doggo's light source in mind while adding shadows here. The light is hitting his left shoulder, creating bright highlights.

HOW TO DRAW:
LOVE RANGER

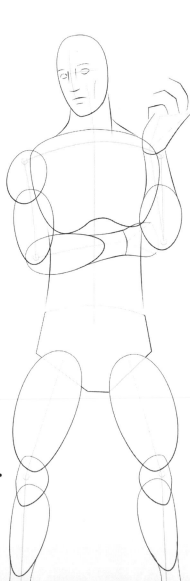

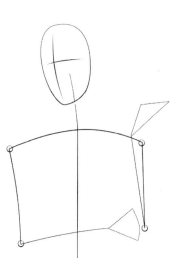

2

Add shape to the body. Loosely sketch the position of Love Ranger's fingers, noting the slight bend in each knuckle. Add the outline of his facial features, including the indent on his cheek.

1

Strike fear into the hearts of your enemies with this Legendary Outfit. Sketch a rough framework of your character, his head facing right.

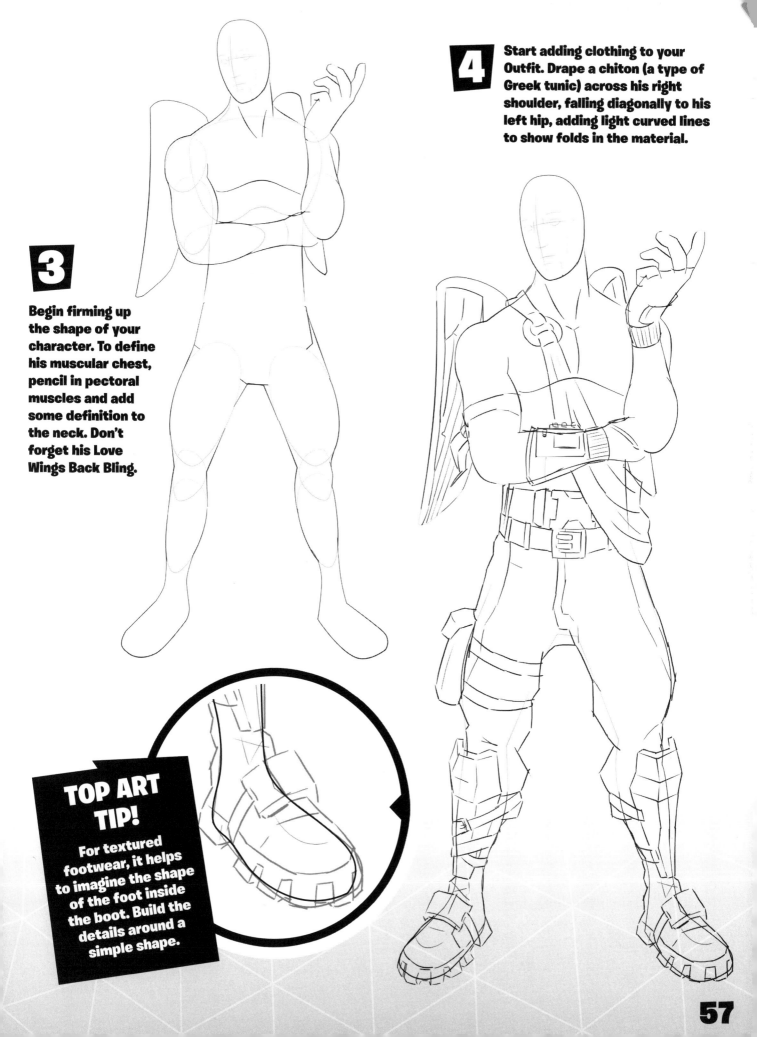

4

Start adding clothing to your Outfit. Drape a chiton (a type of Greek tunic) across his right shoulder, falling diagonally to his left hip, adding light curved lines to show folds in the material.

3

Begin firming up the shape of your character. To define his muscular chest, pencil in pectoral muscles and add some definition to the neck. Don't forget his Love Wings Back Bling.

TOP ART TIP!

For textured footwear, it helps to imagine the shape of the foot inside the boot. Build the details around a simple shape.

HOW TO DRAW: LOVE RANGER

5 Using your guides, draw Love Ranger's chiseled looks. Use light strokes to draw his hair. To add texture, add short, curved lines within the main body of his hair.

TOP ART TIP!

Use short, hard, uneven lines to create the distressed carvings in Love Ranger's chest and shoulders and the cracks in his wings. Draw parallel lines to create the illusion of deeper cracks.

Use thick lines to firmly mark your character's final shape and add cracks to his torso. Since he's made of stone, you don't have to be too careful making your lines neat here.

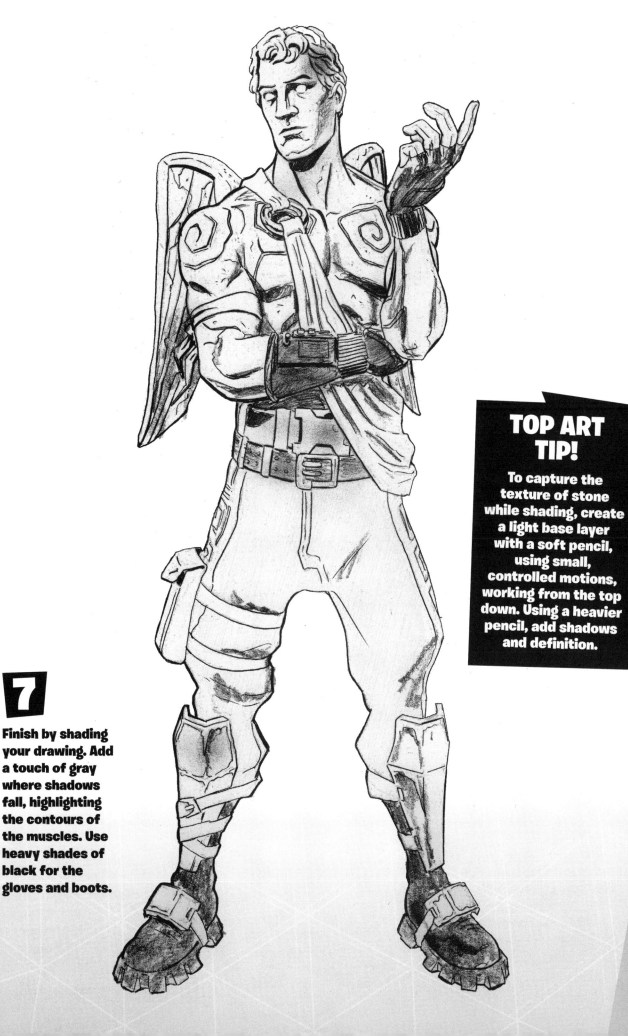

TOP ART TIP!

To capture the texture of stone while shading, create a light base layer with a soft pencil, using small, controlled motions, working from the top down. Using a heavier pencil, add shadows and definition.

7

Finish by shading your drawing. Add a touch of gray where shadows fall, highlighting the contours of the muscles. Use heavy shades of black for the gloves and boots.

HOW TO DRAW:
CATALYST

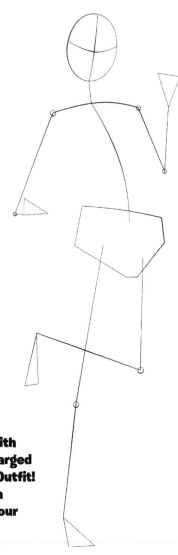

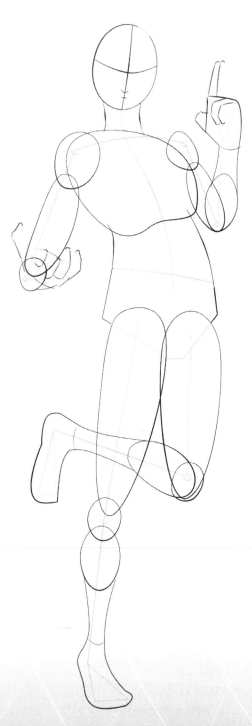

1
Alter the paradigm with this overcharged Legendary Outfit! Begin with a sketch of your character's framework.

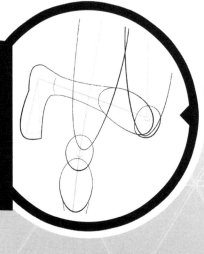

TOP ART TIP!
Although part of Catalyst's raised leg will be covered, it's useful to sketch the full outline to ensure proportions and placement are correct.

2
Build upon your initial sketch, adding shape to the body. Notice how the bends in Catalyst's stance impact the size and length of your base ovals.

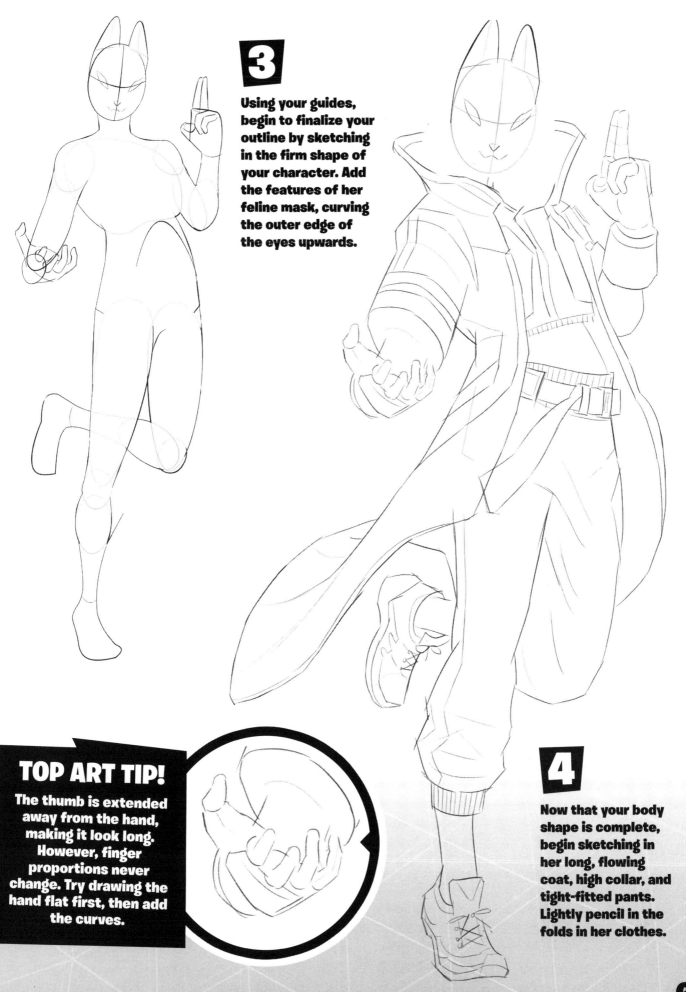

3

Using your guides, begin to finalize your outline by sketching in the firm shape of your character. Add the features of her feline mask, curving the outer edge of the eyes upwards.

TOP ART TIP!

The thumb is extended away from the hand, making it look long. However, finger proportions never change. Try drawing the hand flat first, then add the curves.

4

Now that your body shape is complete, begin sketching in her long, flowing coat, high collar, and tight-fitted pants. Lightly pencil in the folds in her clothes.

HOW TO DRAW: CATALYST

5 Give her mask a more feline shape, using long diagonal lines around the jaw. Triangles and diamonds make for simple features. Now add a spark of electricity!

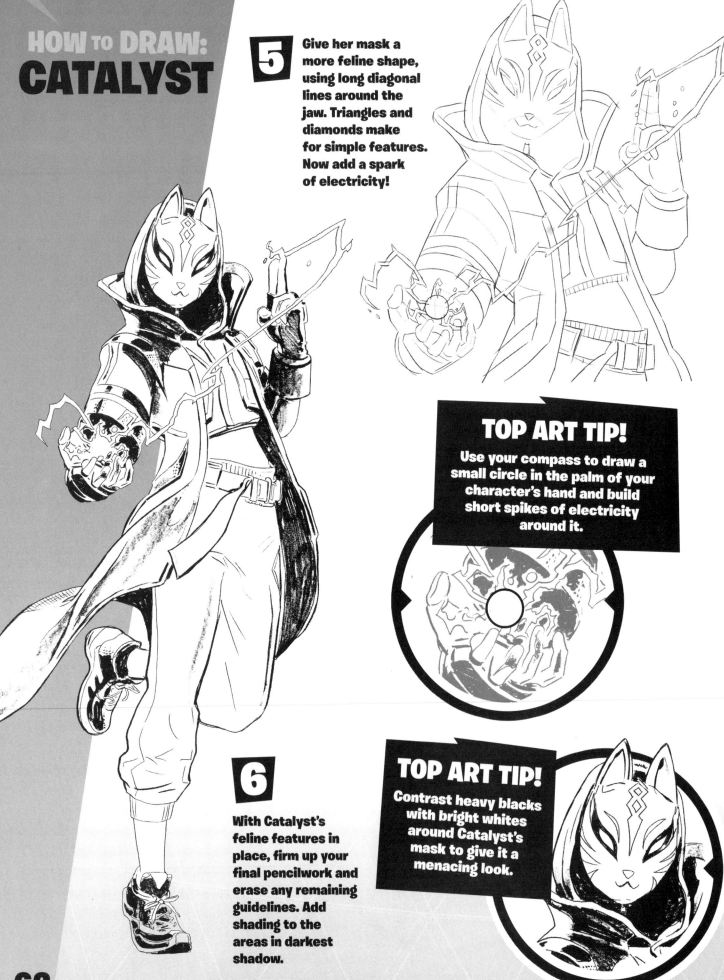

TOP ART TIP!

Use your compass to draw a small circle in the palm of your character's hand and build short spikes of electricity around it.

6 With Catalyst's feline features in place, firm up your final pencilwork and erase any remaining guidelines. Add shading to the areas in darkest shadow.

TOP ART TIP!

Contrast heavy blacks with bright whites around Catalyst's mask to give it a menacing look.

7

Finish by shading your figure. Use a soft, sharp pencil on its side to create thick, black strokes.

TOP ART TIP!

Use crosshatching when shading the outer rim of Catalyst's coat to capture the curve and give it a more interesting texture.

HOW TO DRAW: BLACKHEART

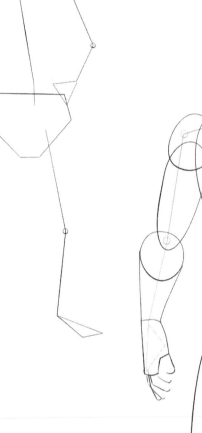

 1 Begin this Legendary Outfit by lightly sketching your character's framework.

TOP ART TIP!
Try not to grip your pencil too tightly when you're sketching. Not only will lines be harder to erase later, but you will tire out your drawing hand quickly.

2 Add shape to your Scallywag. Notice how his shoulders widely arch down and his head tilts forward to create his relaxed stance.

3 With Blackheart's shape in place, create a solid outline of his body. Flesh out the shape of his fingers on his open right hand.

4 Create the shape of his long coat and high boots. Although his pants are baggy, add an indent at the back of his left leg to mark the position of his knee. Add lots of belts, buckles, and patches.

TOP ART TIP!

Hoods react to movement, so don't worry about creating precise lines. Start with the hood's inner lines, considering how it will sit around your character's face, with simple flowing lines around the outside.

HOW TO DRAW: BLACKHEART

5

Although Blackheart's right eye is covered, lightly sketching its placement will help you accurately place his eyepatch. Draw his facial hair, with his beard giving his chin a pointed look.

TOP ART TIP!

While Blackheart's tattoo is partially hidden, using a drawing compass will give the visible part of the circle a clean look.

6

Firm up your outlines and erase any visible rough lines. Begin polishing the finer details and use solid, heavy blacks in the Outfit's darkest areas, including Blackheart's eyepatch and facial hair.

TOP ART TIP!

Using a wide range of values makes your drawing pop. Try experimenting with pencil weight, grip, and pressure to see the different effects.

7

Before setting sail for adventure, add value to your Outfit. Use your eraser to create spots of bright white, adding a shine to Blackheart's leather coat.

HOW TO DRAW:
FISHSTICK

1 Have fun using fluid lines rather than sketching a rigid figure when creating your framework for this Rare Outfit.

TOP ART TIP!

Although Fishstick's body shape is quite human, there are some distinct differences. Take care when sketching his calves, the tilt of his neck and bend of his arm to keep proportions in check.

2 Start adding shape to your character's body. Fishstick doesn't have distinct elbows, so fully curve his right arm as it reaches to his head.

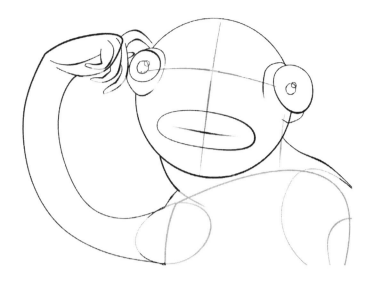

3 Begin adding detail to Fishstick's face. Use your guidelines to help place his wideset eyes. Draw a long oval shape for his mouth. The thick curve of his neck flows directly into his shoulders.

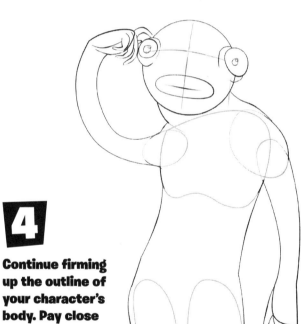

5 It's time to add Fishstick's clothing. Add the belt around his waist and lightly pencil in the creases of his bodysuit. Notice how the fabric falls around his hips and legs.

4 Continue firming up the outline of your character's body. Pay close attention to Fishstick's feet. They are very slim with a defined bend in the sole and curled toes. Hold your pencil in a loose grip to create relaxed waves.

TOP ART TIP!
Since Fishstick's clothing is quite tight-fitted, the wrinkles are simple and pulling into the center of his body. Draw bigger folds in materials for looser-fitting clothes.

6

Begin firming up your pencilwork, erasing any visible guidelines. To create a full fishy effect, lightly add scales to his body.

TOP ART TIP!

Short, simple curved lines is an easy way to draw scales. You don't need to use lots of them. Small patches of four or five lines is an effective way to create the look!

TOP ART TIP!

Fishstick's hat is tight-fitting. Use light hatching to show the outline of his head and gently curve the central stitching line to add dimension. Create the knot at the top by drawing an upside-down prism.

TOP ART TIP!
Define the folds in Fishstick's clothing by adding shadows under each crease, using light circular motions with your pencil.

7

Working from the top down, finish by shading a light-gray base tone over the Outfit. Then define your shadows with a heavy gray and use your eraser to create highlights.

HOW TO DRAW: CRITERION

1 Capture Criterion's unwavering dedication with this Legendary Outfit. Start with a loose sketch of your character.

TOP ART TIP!

Foreshortening is a useful technique to master for drawing figures. The farther away body parts are from you, the shorter their shapes should be. This will give your drawing a realistic look with lots of depth.

2 Draw in the base shape of your character's body. Notice the distinct bend in Criterion's elbows. Although part of her foot is covered, it is useful to lightly sketch the shape.

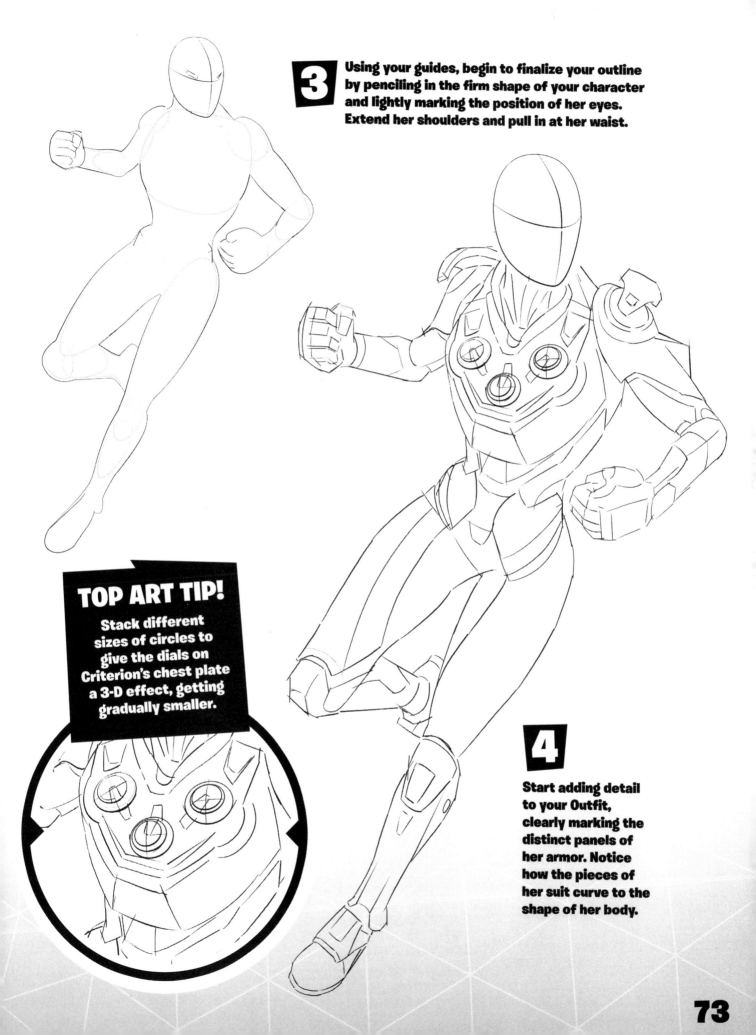

3 Using your guides, begin to finalize your outline by penciling in the firm shape of your character and lightly marking the position of her eyes. Extend her shoulders and pull in at her waist.

TOP ART TIP!

Stack different sizes of circles to give the dials on Criterion's chest plate a 3-D effect, getting gradually smaller.

4

Start adding detail to your Outfit, clearly marking the distinct panels of her armor. Notice how the pieces of her suit curve to the shape of her body.

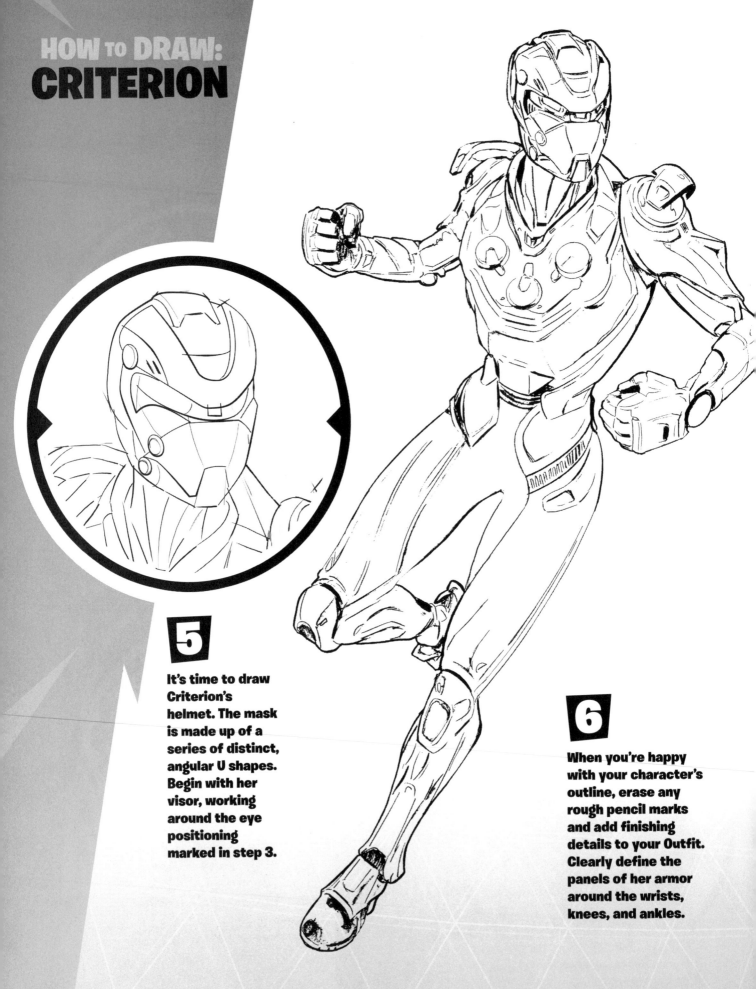

5

It's time to draw Criterion's helmet. The mask is made up of a series of distinct, angular U shapes. Begin with her visor, working around the eye positioning marked in step 3.

6

When you're happy with your character's outline, erase any rough pencil marks and add finishing details to your Outfit. Clearly define the panels of her armor around the wrists, knees, and ankles.

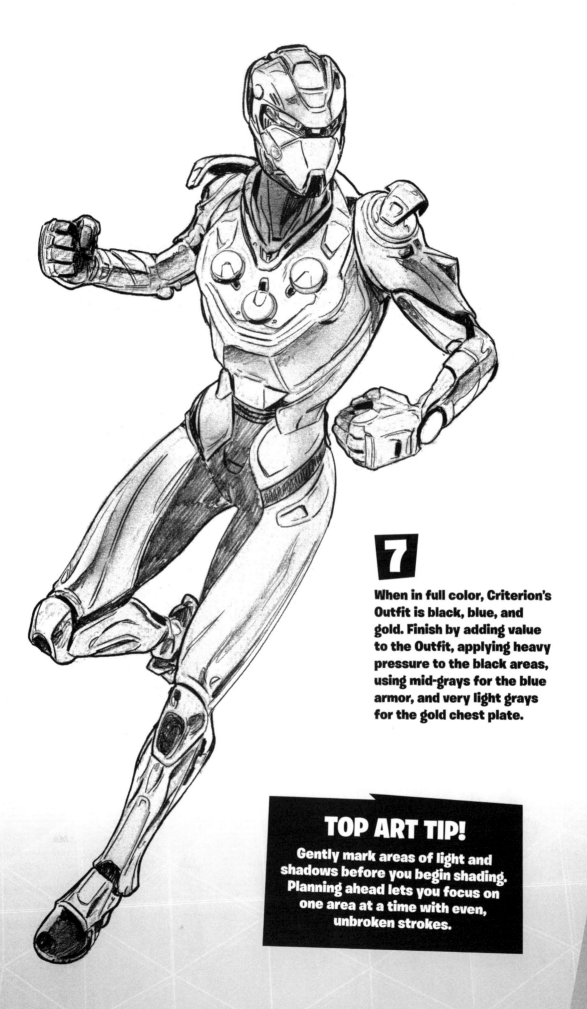

7

When in full color, Criterion's Outfit is black, blue, and gold. Finish by adding value to the Outfit, applying heavy pressure to the black areas, using mid-grays for the blue armor, and very light grays for the gold chest plate.

TOP ART TIP!

Gently mark areas of light and shadows before you begin shading. Planning ahead lets you focus on one area at a time with even, unbroken strokes.

HOW TO DRAW:
OMEGA

1 Start drawing this Legendary Outfit by lightly sketching a framework. Tilt the head forward slightly to capture Omega's menacing pose.

2

Add shape to Omega's body. His fists are tightly clenched here. Carefully consider each finger's positioning. It can help to look at your own hand for reference!

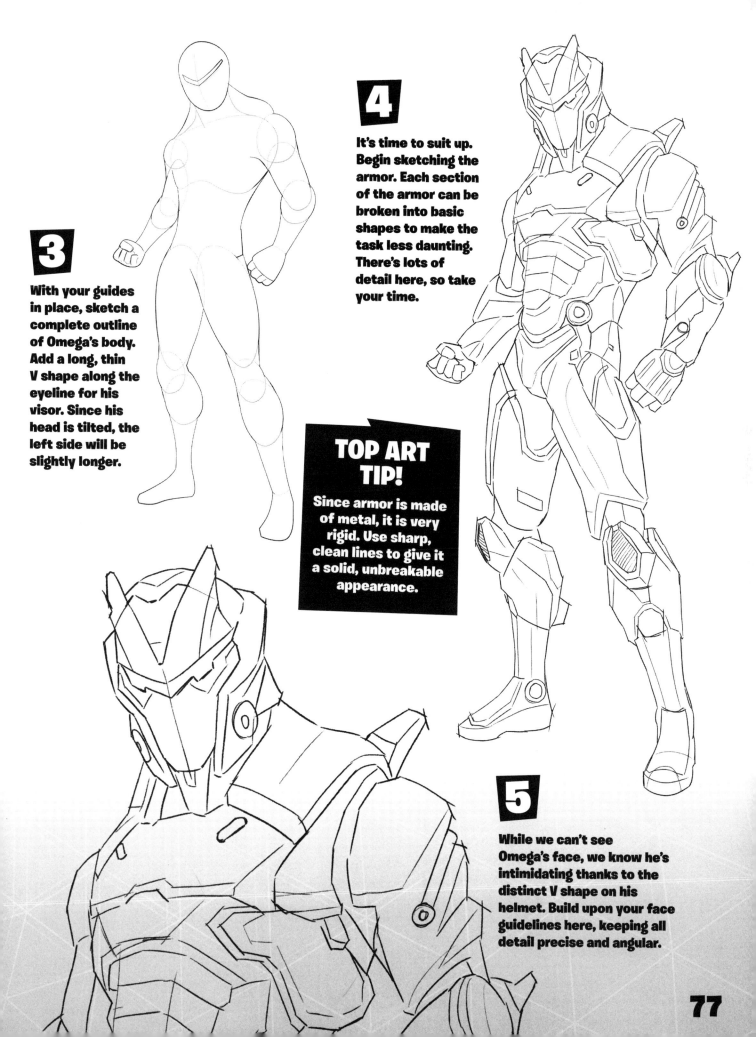

3

With your guides in place, sketch a complete outline of Omega's body. Add a long, thin V shape along the eyeline for his visor. Since his head is tilted, the left side will be slightly longer.

4

It's time to suit up. Begin sketching the armor. Each section of the armor can be broken into basic shapes to make the task less daunting. There's lots of detail here, so take your time.

TOP ART TIP!

Since armor is made of metal, it is very rigid. Use sharp, clean lines to give it a solid, unbreakable appearance.

5

While we can't see Omega's face, we know he's intimidating thanks to the distinct V shape on his helmet. Build upon your face guidelines here, keeping all detail precise and angular.

6

With your armor's detail in place, use thick blacks to outline your character. Mark the darkest areas of shadow with firm, heavy shading.

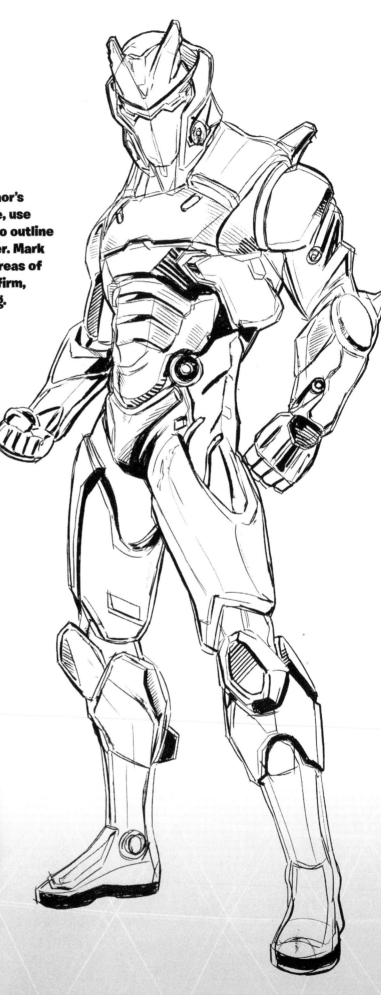

TOP ART TIP!

Use light hatching to add texture and depth to your Outfit. Vary the weight of your strokes and the distance between each line. Hold your pencil at an angle to create thicker lines.

TOP ART TIP!
Shading in small patches rather than long, solid, unified lines helps to define shape and create texture.

7

Finish by adding value to your drawing. It might be tempting to use solid dark blacks for Omega, but high-contrast shading is much more effective!

HOW TO DRAW: CALAMITY

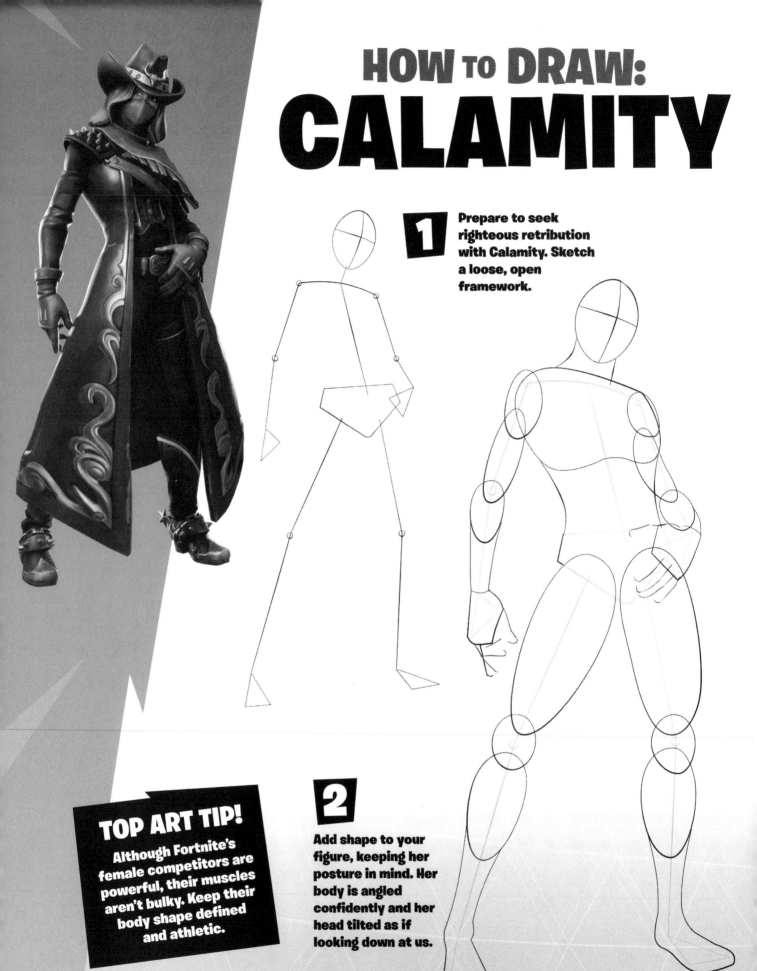

1 Prepare to seek righteous retribution with Calamity. Sketch a loose, open framework.

TOP ART TIP!

Although Fortnite's female competitors are powerful, their muscles aren't bulky. Keep their body shape defined and athletic.

2 Add shape to your figure, keeping her posture in mind. Her body is angled confidently and her head tilted as if looking down at us.

80

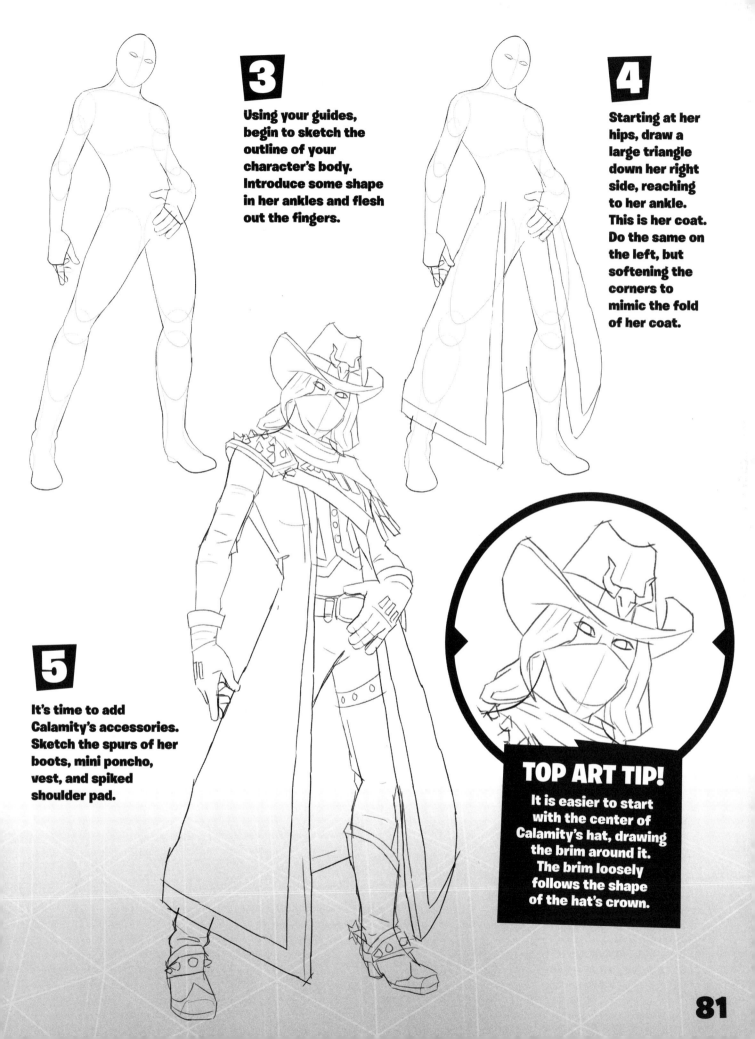

3

Using your guides, begin to sketch the outline of your character's body. Introduce some shape in her ankles and flesh out the fingers.

4

Starting at her hips, draw a large triangle down her right side, reaching to her ankle. This is her coat. Do the same on the left, but softening the corners to mimic the fold of her coat.

5

It's time to add Calamity's accessories. Sketch the spurs of her boots, mini poncho, vest, and spiked shoulder pad.

TOP ART TIP!

It is easier to start with the center of Calamity's hat, drawing the brim around it. The brim loosely follows the shape of the hat's crown.

6 Firm up your outlines and erase any visible guidelines. Use light pencil strokes to add detail to the different layers of clothing.

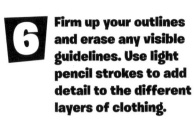

TOP ART TIP!

Draw a series of small cones to create the spikes on Calamity's shoulder pad. They will sit at different angles to help define the curve of her shoulder.

TOP ART TIP!

The embroidery on Calamity's coat looks fancy but is really a curvy W. Start by drawing the letter's outline, curling the ends.

7

Finish by adding value to the darkest areas of your Outfit. Only a light touch of shading is needed where shadows fall. You're ready to head out into the Western Wilds!

HOW TO DRAW:
8-BALL

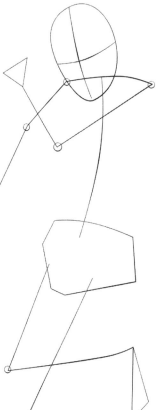

1

Get ready to strike lucky with 8-Ball. Sketch a light framework. This drawing will put your eye for proportions to the test!

TOP ART TIP!

For characters who are posed mid-action, always start your frame with the body's center line. This will capture the "shape" of the movement and the rest of the pose can be structured around it.

2

Begin adding shape to your Outfit. Notice 8-Ball's hunched shoulders and downward tilt of his head, completely covering his neck.

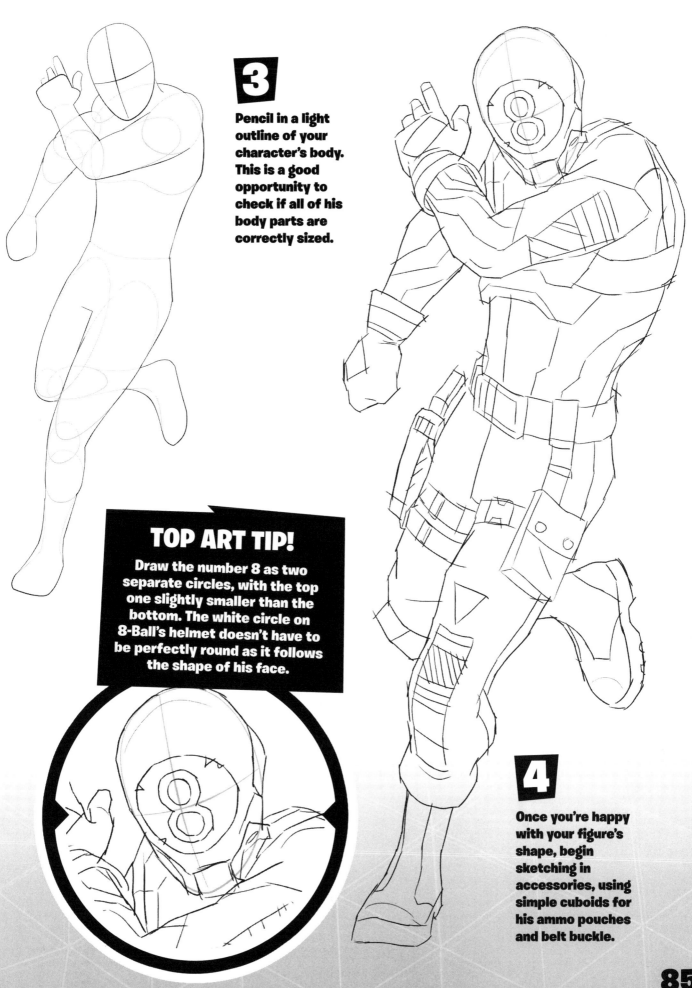

3

Pencil in a light outline of your character's body. This is a good opportunity to check if all of his body parts are correctly sized.

TOP ART TIP!

Draw the number 8 as two separate circles, with the top one slightly smaller than the bottom. The white circle on 8-Ball's helmet doesn't have to be perfectly round as it follows the shape of his face.

4

Once you're happy with your figure's shape, begin sketching in accessories, using simple cuboids for his ammo pouches and belt buckle.

5 Use thick lines to firmly mark 8-Ball's final shape. Erase any remaining guidelines, then lightly pencil in wrinkles in the pant legs.

TOP ART TIP!

Break the symbols on 8-Ball's leg down into basic 2-D shapes: a triangle, two rectangles, and three squares. Keep perspective in mind when adding the detail. The final squares will be slightly smaller.

TOP ART TIP!

Rotating your page can sometimes help with perspective and positioning. Although 8-Ball's leg is raised, the shape of his foot remains the same as if it were flat on the ground.

6

Finish by adding value to this Epic Outfit, transitioning gradually from dark areas to light. 8-Ball's helmet should be as shiny as a real pool ball, so use thick, dark blacks contrasted with patches of bright white to give it a winning glow.

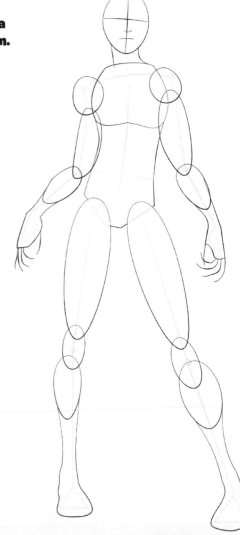

HOW TO DRAW:
THE ICE QUEEN

1 Start drawing this cool Legendary Outfit by sketching a loose framework fit for a queen.

TOP ART TIP!

Female bodies are (usually) much less angular than male bodies. While male figures have broad shoulders and narrow hips, women have wider hips, keeping in line with their shoulders.

2 Build upon your initial sketch, adding shape to the body. The Ice Queen's legs are long and straight, but her upper body is curved and her chin tilted upwards.

3

Using your guides, begin to pencil in the final outline of your character's body. The Ice Queen has large, lemon-shaped eyes. Sketch in their shape here.

4

Lightly sketch The Ice Queen's corset, crown, and feathered coat. To create the clawed effect of her gloves, stack two cylinders for each finger with a cone at the tip.

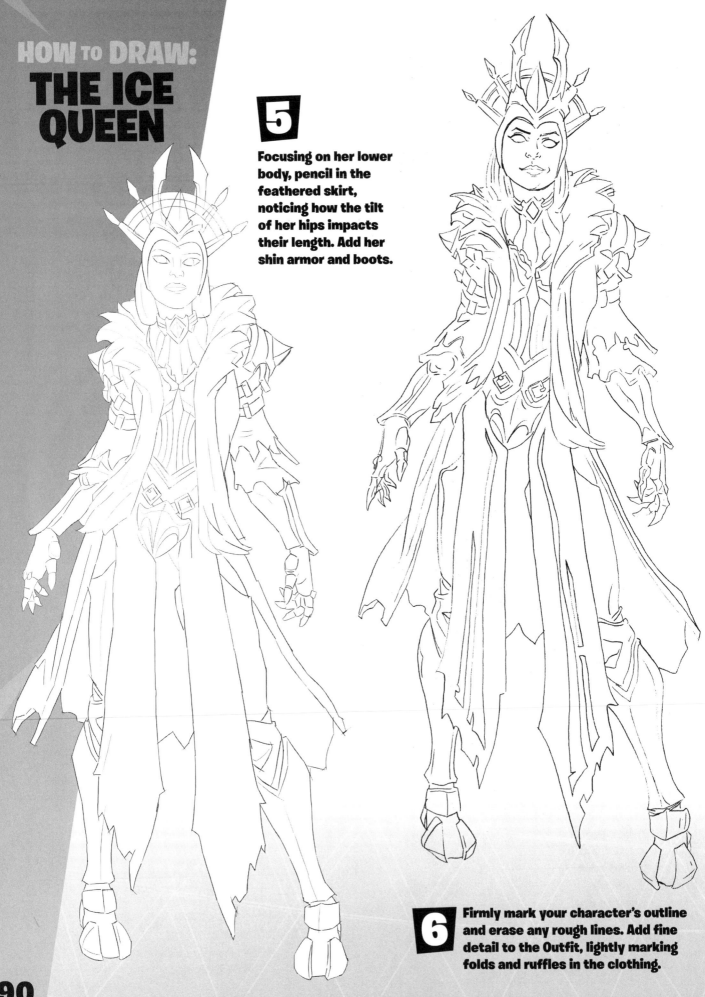

HOW TO DRAW: THE ICE QUEEN

5

Focusing on her lower body, pencil in the feathered skirt, noticing how the tilt of her hips impacts their length. Add her shin armor and boots.

6

Firmly mark your character's outline and erase any rough lines. Add fine detail to the Outfit, lightly marking folds and ruffles in the clothing.

7

Shade your drawing, using the side of your pencil to transition from light to dark. This will create a chilling transition effect. For thick blacks, apply heavier pressure on your pencil.

HOW TO DRAW:
RIPPLEY

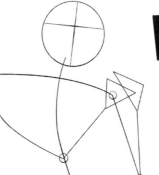

1 Begin your drippy and dangerous drawing of Rippley by sketching a loose framework.

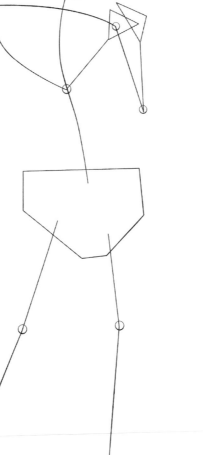

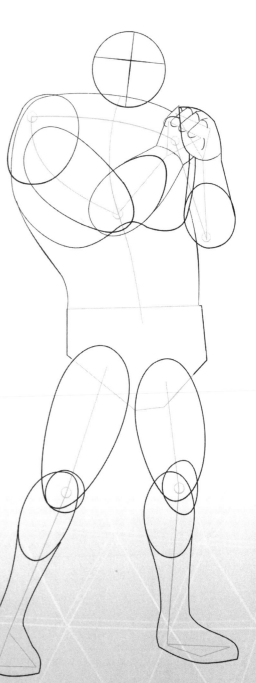

TOP ART TIP!

Because he's made of Slurp Juice, Rippley's hands don't curve quite like human hands do. When drawing his tight-fisted pose, keep his fists rounded, with no knuckles to define shape in his fingers.

2 Start adding shape to your character. Take care to define Rippley's perfectly round head and broad shoulders. Pull his waist in slightly to emphasize his large upper body.

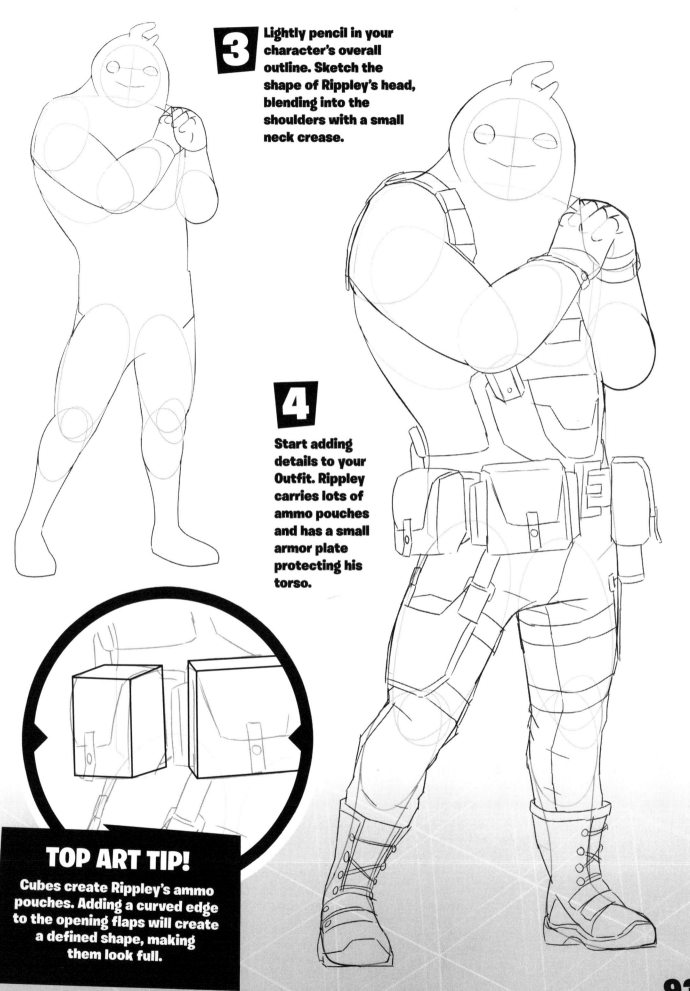

3 Lightly pencil in your character's overall outline. Sketch the shape of Rippley's head, blending into the shoulders with a small neck crease.

4

Start adding details to your Outfit. Rippley carries lots of ammo pouches and has a small armor plate protecting his torso.

TOP ART TIP!

Cubes create Rippley's ammo pouches. Adding a curved edge to the opening flaps will create a defined shape, making them look full.

HOW TO DRAW:
RIPPLEY

5

Add the finishing details to Rippley and his uniform. Lightly draw small spots on the liquid part of his body. When shaded, these will give your Outfit a watery texture.

6

Finish by laying down a light-gray base tone, keeping it particularly soft around the face. Add darker value to the gloves, boots, and pouches, and a light touch of shading in shadowy areas. Leave a few bright-white spots on Rippley's upper body to give him a Slurp Juice shine!

TOP ART TIP!

Defining your light source is particularly important when shading liquid. Shadows usually fall where large areas of liquid concentrate.

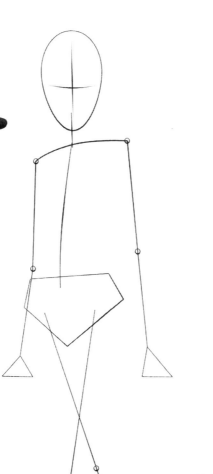

HOW TO DRAW: LYNX

1

Level up with this top-tier Legendary Outfit. Begin by sketching a loose framework, noting the position of Lynx's legs and the light curve in her torso.

2

Start adding shape to her body. Add simple lines for her long, curved tail and her outstretched fingers. Lightly sketch placement for her chest armor.

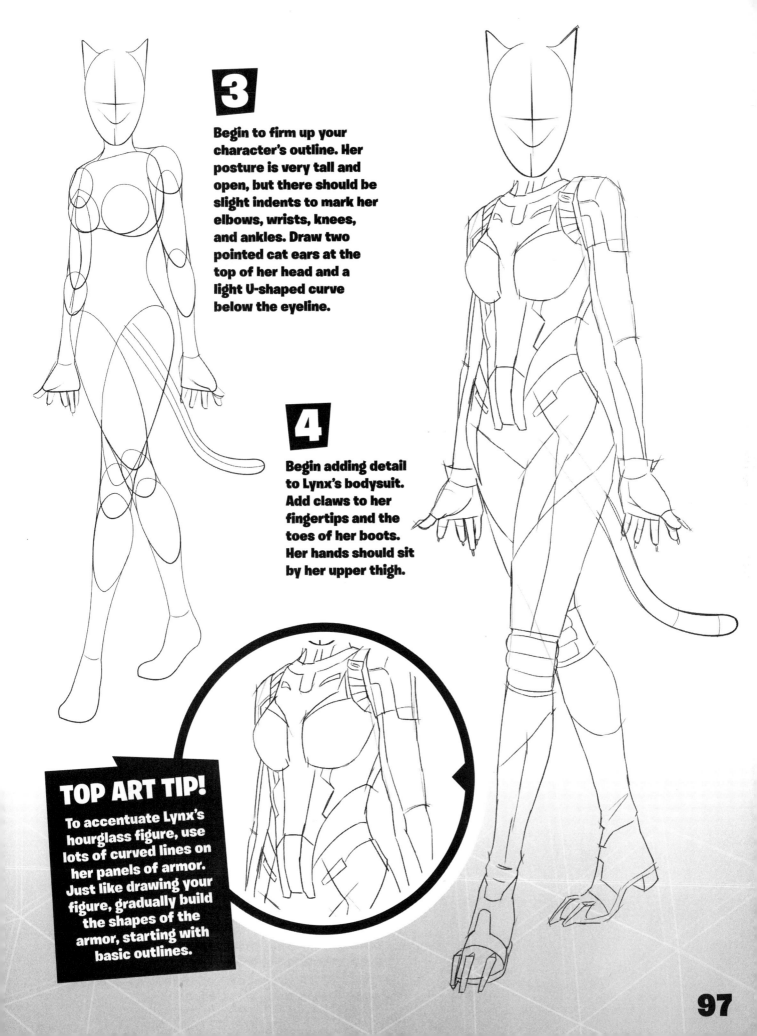

3

Begin to firm up your character's outline. Her posture is very tall and open, but there should be slight indents to mark her elbows, wrists, knees, and ankles. Draw two pointed cat ears at the top of her head and a light U-shaped curve below the eyeline.

4

Begin adding detail to Lynx's bodysuit. Add claws to her fingertips and the toes of her boots. Her hands should sit by her upper thigh.

TOP ART TIP!

To accentuate Lynx's hourglass figure, use lots of curved lines on her panels of armor. Just like drawing your figure, gradually build the shapes of the armor, starting with basic outlines.

97

HOW TO DRAW: LYNX

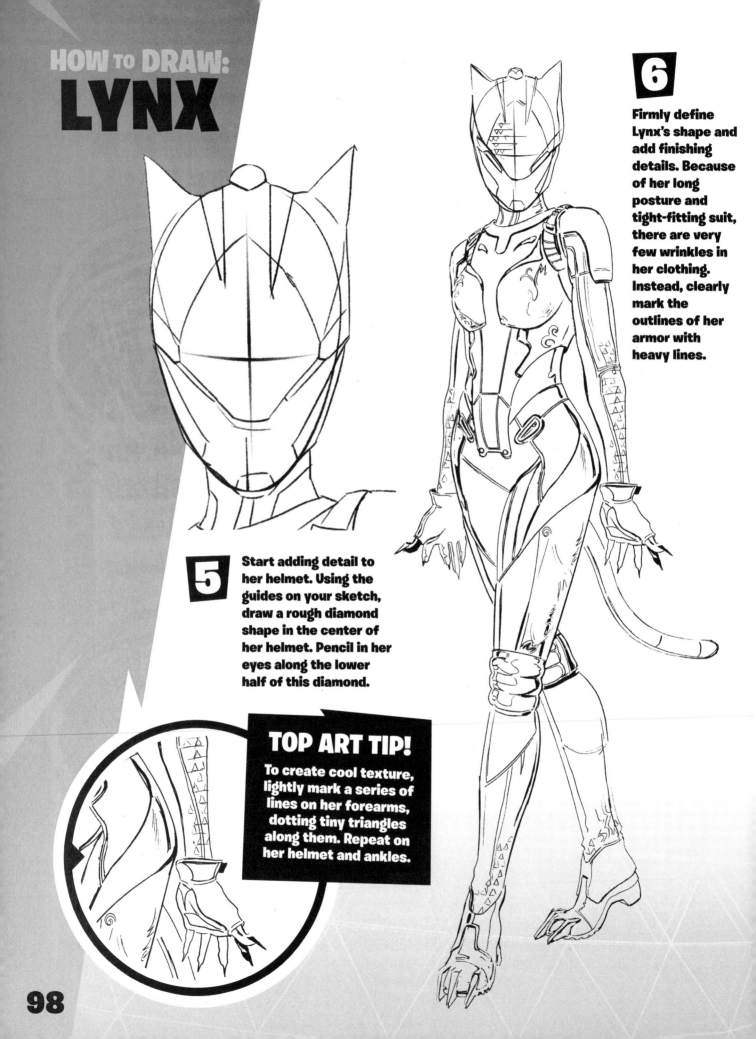

6

Firmly define Lynx's shape and add finishing details. Because of her long posture and tight-fitting suit, there are very few wrinkles in her clothing. Instead, clearly mark the outlines of her armor with heavy lines.

5

Start adding detail to her helmet. Using the guides on your sketch, draw a rough diamond shape in the center of her helmet. Pencil in her eyes along the lower half of this diamond.

TOP ART TIP!

To create cool texture, lightly mark a series of lines on her forearms, dotting tiny triangles along them. Repeat on her helmet and ankles.

7

Finally, add value to your Outfit. Lynx's armor gradually gets darker from top to bottom. Start at the top and work your way down to avoid smudging. This high-contrast shading will really make your drawing stand out!

99

HOW TO DRAW:
A.I.M.

1

Start drawing this Legendary Outfit by lightly sketching A.I.M.'s framework.

2 Add shape to your sketch. Although A.I.M. isn't a human character, his build is similar to a male figure's.

3 Carefully sketch in blocky, robotic shapes. Begin with simple cubes and cylinders, then play with angles for a more defined shape.

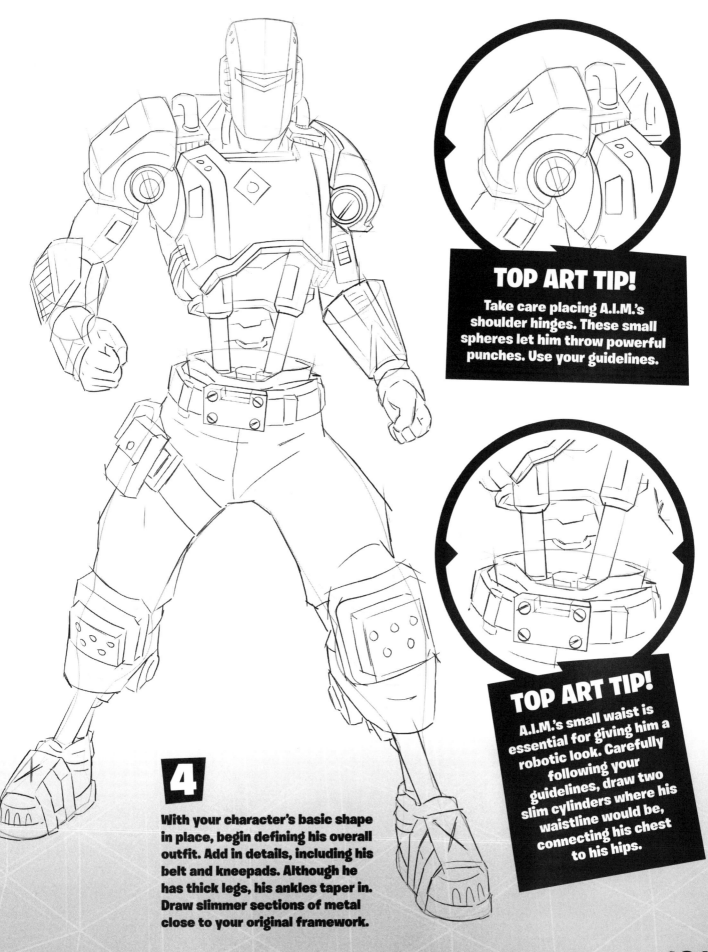

TOP ART TIP!

Take care placing A.I.M.'s shoulder hinges. These small spheres let him throw powerful punches. Use your guidelines.

TOP ART TIP!

A.I.M.'s small waist is essential for giving him a robotic look. Carefully following your guidelines, draw two slim cylinders where his waistline would be, connecting his chest to his hips.

4

With your character's basic shape in place, begin defining his overall outfit. Add in details, including his belt and kneepads. Although he has thick legs, his ankles taper in. Draw slimmer sections of metal close to your original framework.

HOW TO DRAW:
A.I.M.

TOP ART TIP!

The center of A.I.M.'s kneepad is simply a small cube stacked on top of a larger cube.

TOP ART TIP!

A.I.M.'s forearm closely follows a long cylinder shape, thick at the elbow and tapering in at the wrist.

Firmly pencil in A.I.M.'s outline, taking care to define the details of his gadgets. Use a ruler for a mechanical look.

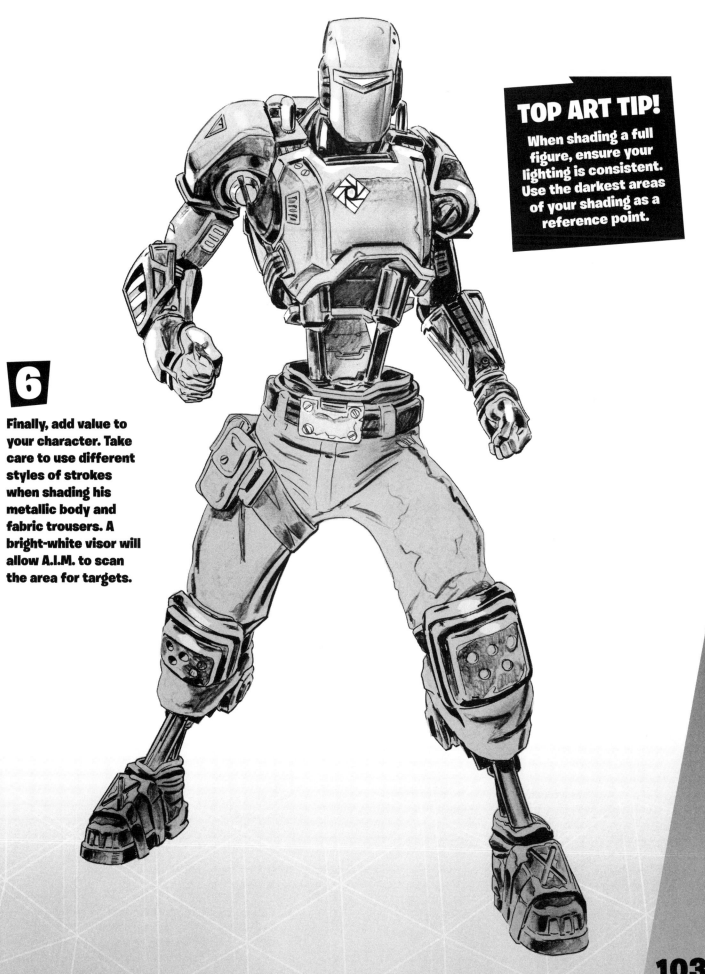

TOP ART TIP!

When shading a full figure, ensure your lighting is consistent. Use the darkest areas of your shading as a reference point.

6

Finally, add value to your character. Take care to use different styles of strokes when shading his metallic body and fabric trousers. A bright-white visor will allow A.I.M. to scan the area for targets.

HOW TO DRAW:
DARK VOYAGER

Take on the galaxy with this Legendary Outfit. Sketch a framework for your body.

2

Flesh out your framework, giving your character more shape. Note the bend in the left elbow. Dark Voyager's hand should reach to the center of his torso.

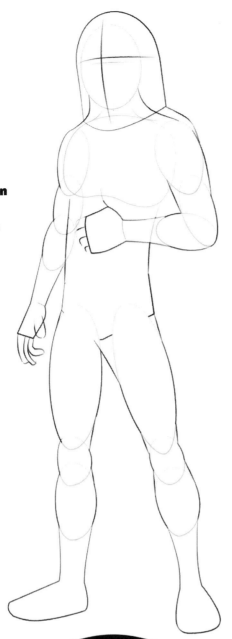

3

Lightly pencil in an outline of your character's body. Instead of drawing a face, sketch a large dome around the head of your framework, extending your facial guides to help keep things in proportion.

TOP ART TIP!

Dark Voyager's helmet isn't a simple circle shape, but it can be broken down into a series of curved lines, layered on top of one another.

4

Start adding detail to your Outfit, working from the top down and focusing on one section at a time. Use wide crosshatching to create texture in the panel on the side of his suit.

5 Begin to firm up your pencil lines and add finer details to the Outfit. Erase any remaining rough lines.

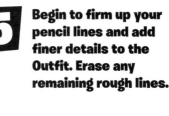

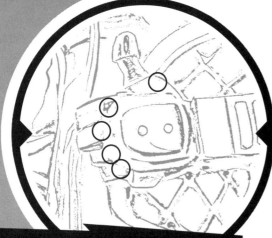

TOP ART TIP!

Knuckles aren't perfectly stacked in the thumbs-up pose. Notice how the middle finger protrudes slightly. The thumb curves slightly around its knuckles. Draw an exaggerated tip around the thumb to capture the thickness of the glove.

TOP ART TIP!

Dark Voyager's gadgets look complicated, but are really made up of lots of cuboids, like this radio. Try breaking difficult Outfit elements down into simpler shapes.

6

Finally, add value to your character, playing with various shades of gray, keeping the glowing panels light. Use heavy shading for the helmet's visor, contouring your lines to make your helmet look curved. Leave one bright-white spot for an effective contrast.

HOW TO DRAW: WUKONG

1

To draw this Legendary monkey king, start with a loose framework.

2

Begin to flesh out your character. Wukong's face should be longer than a standard human's, with the eyeline running through the middle. This will help you place his crown.

TOP ART TIP!

Wukong's thick armor will impact the size of his outline. Draw your body's outline farther away from the framework to allow more space for the bulk of his armor!

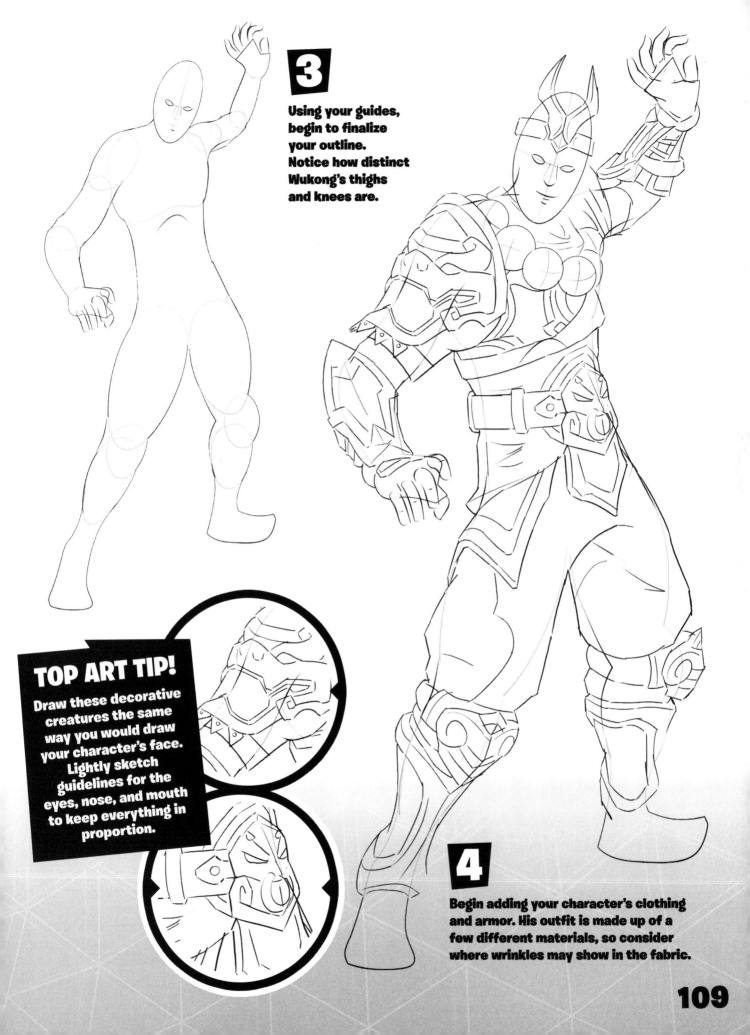

3

Using your guides, begin to finalize your outline. Notice how distinct Wukong's thighs and knees are.

TOP ART TIP!

Draw these decorative creatures the same way you would draw your character's face. Lightly sketch guidelines for the eyes, nose, and mouth to keep everything in proportion.

4

Begin adding your character's clothing and armor. His outfit is made up of a few different materials, so consider where wrinkles may show in the fabric.

HOW TO DRAW: WUKONG

5

Define Wukong's facial features and draw the outline of his hair. Long hair falls in sections. Working from the top down, draw long sections using uneven, overlapping pencil strokes.

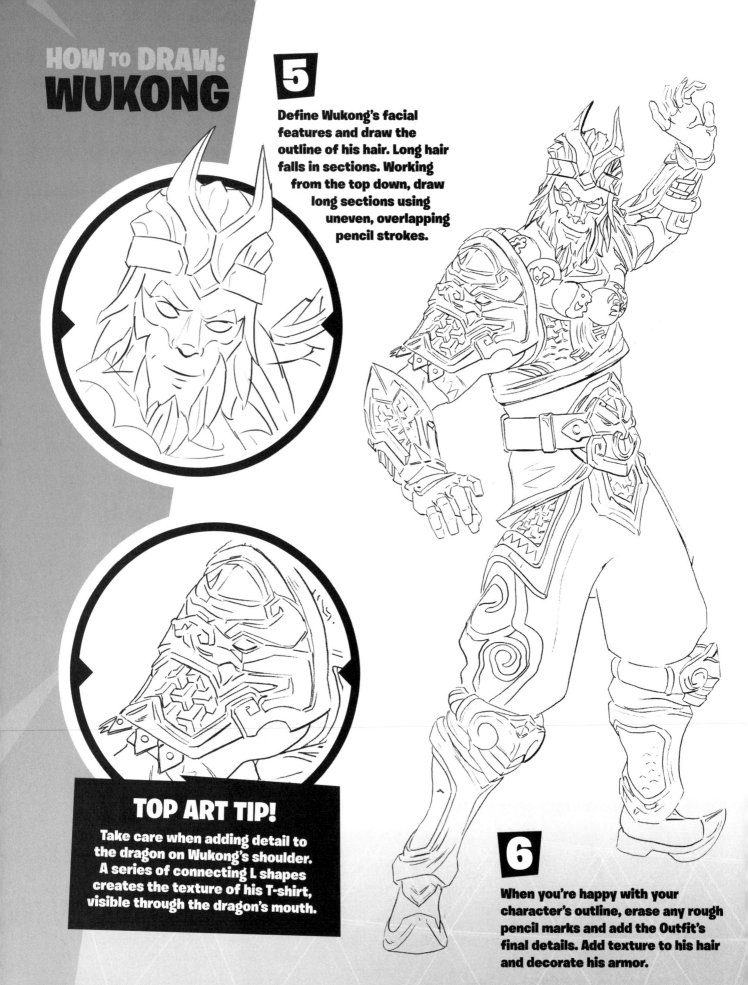

TOP ART TIP!

Take care when adding detail to the dragon on Wukong's shoulder. A series of connecting L shapes creates the texture of his T-shirt, visible through the dragon's mouth.

6

When you're happy with your character's outline, erase any rough pencil marks and add the Outfit's final details. Add texture to his hair and decorate his armor.

7

Finish by adding value to your drawing. Wukong's Outfit is made up of gold armor and fabric. Use different shading techniques to portray the different materials. Light grays and whites will give the gold armor an impressive shine!

First published in the UK in 2020 by WILDFIRE an imprint of HEADLINE PUBLISHING GROUP

Cataloguing in Publication Data is available from the British Library

Paperback 978 14722 7244 7

Written by Kirsten Murray

Illustrations by Mike Collins

Design by Amazing15

All images © Epic Games, Inc.

Printed and bound in Slovenia

HEADLINE PUBLISHING GROUP
An Hachette UK Company
Carmelite House
50 Victoria Embankment
London, EC4 0DZ
www.headline.co.uk www.hachette.co.uk

Little, Brown and Company
Hachette Book Group
1290 Avenue of the Americas, New York, NY 10104
Visit us at hbgusa.com/fortnite

www.epicgames.com

First Edition: June 2020

First U.S. Edition: July 2020

Little, Brown and Company is a division of Hachette Book Group, Inc.

The Little, Brown name and logo are trademarks of Hachette Book Group, Inc.

ISBN: 978-0-316-70406-9 (pbk), 978-0-316-59142-3 (ebook), 978-0-316-59141-6 (ebook), 978-0-316-59139-3 (ebook)

U.S. edition printed in the United States of America

All images © Epic Games, Inc.

CW
UK: 10 9 8 7 6 5 4 3 2 1
U.S.: 10 9 8 7 6 5 4 3 2